SMART
CHOICES

July '03

Ted,

Thanks so much
for your kind
words.

Best wishes
— Matt G

SMART
CHOICES

SELECTING AND
ADMINISTERING
A SAFE 401K PLAN

MATTHEW GNABASIK

BLUE PRAIRIE GROUP, LLC
CHICAGO, IL

SMART CHOICES:
Selecting and Administering a Safe 401k Plan
Copyright © 2002 by Matthew Gnabasik

Published by
Blue Prairie Group, LLC
7311 Quick Avenue
River Forest, IL 60305-1938

Library of Congress Cataloging-in-Publication Data is available for this title.
ISBN: 0-615-12106-3

Blue Prairie books are available at special discounts for bulk purchases by corporations, institutions, and other organizations. For more information, please call 1-866-274-1899, or write Blue Prairie Group at info@blueprairiegroup.com

Please Note: The information provided is intended as general information and should not be construed as legal advice or a legal opinion on any specific facts or circumstances. The information is not intended to be a substitute for obtaining advice from your own accountant, tax professional or legal counsel.

BOOK INTERIOR DESIGNED BY KATHLEEN LAKE, NEUWIRTH AND ASSOCIATES, INC.

10   9   8   7   6   5   4   3   2   1
Printed in the United States of America

This book is dedicated to my parents,
Martin and Patricia Gnabasik.

It is also dedicated to my wife, Gina, and my daughter, Sofia.
Thank you for your love, support and encouragement.

CONTENTS

PART I

PART II

APPENDIX

ACKNOWLEDGMENTS

This book was written over several years. During that time, I received help in ways both large and small from many people. I would like to thank the many generous people who gave of their time and expertise.

First, I'd like to thank past and present clients for the trust they showed in me and the privilege of working with them on their retirement plans.

A heartfelt thanks to the following people who endured the manuscript at various stages of its development and whose thoughtful comments and suggestions made it better: Becky Amato, Kalyn Johnson, Colleen Gnabasik, Diana Pihos, Mike Schwartz, Terri Marrs, Dan Frick, David Hill, Gail Lingle, Bob Ierardi, Todd Smiser, Jerry Ahler, Caroll Iler, Rick Caccamise, Gary Anderson, Ric Gazarian, Mark Ferraro, Steve Scott, and Michael Kane.

Thank you to all the people involved with the various aspects of production and marketing:

Jodee Blanco who served as guide and oversaw the entire project. Kent Carroll (editor), Olga Gardner (copy editor), Andy Carpenter (cover designer), Swordsmith (proofreading), Kathy Lake and Beth Metrick at Neuwirth & Associates (interior design and production), Bind Rite (printing), Jen Linck at Biblio (distribution), and Lissy Peace at Blanco and Peace and Natalie Rofalikos (promotion).

I'd also like to thank Mike Segal and Jim Meyer for their support and assistance in getting this book published.

I am deeply grateful to two people whose tireless assistance in fact checking and proof reading made this book as error-free as possible: Linda Shashinka, employee benefits attorney and Cecilia Brunetti, my colleage.

I could have not written this book without the help of my wife, Gina Latinovich. Not only is she is a crack writer and editor but she served as my sounding board throughout the entire writing process. Thank you.

Such a fact-filled book is bound to contain errors and I take full responsibility for them. If readers spot any, please contact me via e-mail at matt@blueprairiegroup.com.

ONE

INTRODUCTION

✦

Smart Choices: Selecting and Administering a Safe 401(k) Plan will give you a road map to the best retirement plan available today. Whether you're a first-time buyer or considering a change from your current plan provider, following the steps outlined in this book will ensure that you get the best product at the best price in today's marketplace.

This book was created for companies—those that already sponsor a retirement plan as well as those that intend to set one up.[1] This book was also written for "advisors"—the consultants, brokers, accountants and lawyers who often participate in the implementation and maintenance of company-sponsored retirement plans. Even if you choose a retirement plan other than a 401(k), like a 403(b), SEP, 457, or Profit Sharing, this book will serve you well. All the basic information you need—from plan design to government compliance, investments, plan costs, and employee education—is provided.

This book also describes a process that you need to understand if you are responsible for your company's retirement program or if you are an advisor active in this field. Federal laws governing 401(k)s require that you, the buyer, make an *informed* decision based on *procedural due diligence*. This means that if you make a poor buying decision, you can't plead ignorance. When you buy a 401(k) plan, you put employees' retirement funds at risk, and the laws take that very seriously. You must make decisions in the best interests of participants and be able to justify them.

Today's employees know whether their company has a plan and how it stacks up against plans offered by other employers. They are also keeping track of how their retirement funds are doing. Technological innovations made over the past twenty years, such as daily valuation, twenty-four-hour voice response, and Web-based services have "increased the quantity, quality and immediacy of information available to plan participants."[2] Financial news alongside sports and weather has become standard newscast fare. All the popular financial magazines devote at least one issue a year to retirement strategies, with 401(k)s often the lead story. This attention puts pressure on plan sponsors to make well-informed and well-documented buying decisions. And the recent Enron 401(k) scandal spotlights the consequences of making ill-advised decisions.

Over the past two decades, the amount of money in 401(k) accounts has ballooned. According to the Investment Company Institute, the average participant account balance was $55,502 at year-end 2000.[3] The 401(k) average account balance is now roughly equal to the average homeowner's equity—traditionally the single largest component of a person's net worth.[4] With the relative decline of Social Security as a source for retirement funds,[5] 401(k) remains the last best chance for many to achieve their retirement goals. With so much at stake, employees are asking informed questions and demanding satisfactory answers. It's no longer enough to simply offer a 401(k) plan, you must offer a competitive one.

And be prepared for lawsuits.[6] It is a commonly held industry opinion that there will be enormous litigation in the next two decades as baby boomers retire and realize they don't have enough money to maintain their pre-retirement lifestyle. The law requires you to justify your plan decisions and a disgruntled employee may want to know why he doesn't have more money in his account.[7] It's best not to find yourself in this position, and if you educate yourself about retirement plans—fiduciary liability, plan design, investments, etc.—you won't have to. After you buy a 401(k) package, you should feel good about your decision, confident that you have made a choice that's right for your company and your employees.

You should be able to approach your decision as comfortably as you would approach buying a car. A strange analogy? Not really. A 401(k) package is a complex financial, tax, and legal product, and a car is a complex machine, but they're both manmade and both for sale. Making an informed 401(k) buying decision requires sound knowledge. You'll be evaluating options and features and you'll need to differentiate between hype and information. You'll narrow down your choices. And just as in buying a car, there will be features you must have and potential problems you'll want to avoid.

However, there is one big difference. When you buy a car, you have informed sources to help you: your mechanic, the *Blue Book,* and *Consumer Reports.* You can check and double-check your information. When you buy a 401(k), there is a lot more at stake—your own future financial security and that of your employees—yet there is far less good advice available to guide you. If you're buying a new car, you probably know which brands have a good reputation before you even arrive at the dealership. You've thought about what features are important to you in a new car. You might look at the glossy marketing brochures, but you know that they are far from objective. When you are ready to buy, you will have solid facts on which to base your decision.

When you consider buying a 401(k) plan, do you know which plans have the best track record? If you're looking at the marketing brochures, can you separate hype from reality? Do you know how 401(k) plans work, what they should cost, what the marketplace benchmarks are? Do you know, in other words, what you can get for your money? You might look for easy maintenance and good mileage in a new car, but how do you define a "successful" 401(k) plan? How do you select the right vendor? What's a fair price? How do you know if you are fulfilling your fiduciary responsibility? How do you select investments? And to whom can you turn for help?

If you're shopping for a 401(k) plan, remember that the salesperson's job is to sell product and that his job may take precedence over what's best for you and your employees. The vendors—mutual-fund companies, banks, insurers, third-party administrators and brokerage firms that set up and administer 401(k) plans—will be happy to provide information. But just like the glossy marketing brochures, they are rarely objective. Knowledge is power, and the buyer who knows very little about 401(k) makes an easy target for product salespeople.

I spent four years selling 401(k) plans for a large insurance company. In 1996, I became a consultant and since then I've run three retirement plan consulting practices, working with clients around the country. This book began with a stunning realization. Most people buy 401(k)s with very little understanding of what they are buying. (Despite all the press attention given to 401(k) plans, most of the articles are written for plan participants and not for the plan sponsor. There is a real lack of good consolidated information for the plan sponsor.) The idea of this book is simple: if you, the 401(k) buyer, know in advance how these plans work, what you can get for your money, and what's a fair price, then you are far more likely to select the right vendor. You'll also be able to defend your decision better under the pressure of a government audit or, worse, a lawsuit.

Smart Choices is a book written by a professional pension consultant. I have no product to sell—no proprietary investments or record-keeping systems clouding my judgement. As a consultant, I do not represent any one company nor do I have an ax to grind concerning how a plan should be set up. I make my living advising clients on how to design, implement, and maintain the best possible retirement plan for their company. This book is a distillation of over ten years of experience in the field. Most of the information that I'm passing on to you has been acquired the hard way and reflects real world experience.

Smart Choices gives you a map to the best 401(k) for you and your company. If you follow its advice, it will ensure that you employ due diligence in selecting the right vendor for the right reasons. The buyer who uses a proven process can be assured that he will get the best plan for his company at the best price. It doesn't matter if you are starting a plan for the first time or you have an existing plan with $500 million of retirement assets. The steps laid out in this book will lead you to a sound buying decision. You will have done everything required to select the best 401(k) plan for you and your company and you will have documented the process all along the way.

Buying and administering a 401(k) plan may seem at first like a daunting task, but together we can break the process down into manageable pieces. There is information to master but there is a clear path through it. You can make an intelligent, informed decision and be satisfied with a job well done. And that's the best deal for you and your company.

The book is divided into three sections. Part 1, which includes chapters 2 through 6, explains the background of 401(k) plans. Topics include different types of qualified plans, the rise of the mutual fund industry, fiduciary responsibilities, required government testing, and the major elements of plan design.

Part 2, which includes chapters 7 through 13, discusses the component parts of every 401(k) plan, such as recordkeeping, technology, investments, employee education, and plan costs. Other topics include benchmarking and ways to formally market a plan.

Finally, the appendix has useful examples and resources referenced throughout the book.

If you're new to the subject of retirement planning, you might want to read straight through the book. If you've already got a basic knowledge, you can use *Smart Choices* as a reference. Each chapter is designed as a stand-alone unit so if you feel comfortable skipping certain chapters, do so. Unless you're a retirement plan advisor, you probably won't be using the information in this book often enough to commit it to memory. So think of *Smart Choices* as years of experience you can keep on your bookshelf, and remember, the process of selecting and administering the best retirement plan for your company is well within reach.

Notes

1. "It is important to note what small employers without plans do not know about plan sponsorship. Small employers that offer a retirement plan report that offering a plan has a positive impact on both their ability to attract and retain quality employees as well as on the attitude and performance of their employees. The sur-

vey results indicate that many small companies may gain such potential business benefits from plan sponsorship."

"EBRI Retirement Income Research: 2000 Findings," *www.ebri.org,* February 5, 2001.

2. "Defining Value: A Report on Defined Contribution Plans in the Tax-Exempt Sector," Fidelity Investments, 2001, p. 10.

3. Investment Company Institute, *2001 Mutual Funds Fact Book,* Chapter 5, "Mutual Funds and the Retirement Market," p. 6. According to Fidelity, the average account balance in 2000 was $55,000. Building Futures: Volume III, p. 19. The median account balance was $13,493 at year-end 2000, which is 11 percent lower than the median account balance of $15,246 at year-end 1999, but 3 percent higher than the $13,038 median account balance at year-end 1998. EBRI Issue Brief, Number 239, November 2001, p. 14.

4. Median home equity for homeowners' households increased between 1991 and 1993 from $43,070 in 1991 to $46,669 in 1993. Median net worth for households in 1993 was $37,587. (Asset Ownership of Households: 1993, The Survey of Income and Program Participation (SIPP).)

5. The Social Security system is expected to begin running a deficit within only fifteen years (paying out more in benefits than it collects in taxes). Current estimates calculate that, without reform, it will be unable to pay promised benefits starting around 2037.

http://www.socialsecurityreform.org/problem/index.cfm

6. Although the Enron and Global Crossing class action suits are currently receiving most of the headlines, there are always participant-initiated lawsuits taking place. The most common types of lawsuits usually fall into one of the following categories:

- ✦ Advisability of company stock
- ✦ Challenges to blackout periods and mapping techniques
- ✦ Valuation techniques for non-daily valued plans
- ✦ Late or misrouted 401(k) contributions

"401(k) Plan Litigation Under ERISA," Thomas Gigot, *Journal of Pension Planning and Compliance*, Fall 2001.

7. "Thirteen percent of investors polled recently said that they would have to delay retirement because of stock losses. . . . More than 22% of the respondents in the 55-64 age group said they would have to work longer. The proportion rose to one-fourth for those 65 and older." "Retirements Delayed by Losses, Survey Says," *New York Times*, February 17, 2002, Business Section, p.8.

CHAPTER 1

MARKET OVERVIEW

✦

4 01(k) plans are hot. Employees are clamoring for them, employers are setting them up in record numbers, and service providers are tripping over one another to get a piece of the pie.

And what a pie it is! From its humble origins in the early 1980s, 401(k) has become the retirement plan of choice.[1] What accounts for this explosive popularity? First, there has been a seismic shift in the pension landscape in the last twenty years—defined-contribution plans have largely replaced the traditional company-paid pension plans of the past.[2] This move, away from a 100 percent corporate-paid responsibility and toward a shared corporate/individual responsibility, is inseparable from two other related trends we will be examining in this chapter: the growth of 401(k) assets and the advance of the mutual fund industry.

Increasing 401(k) assets and the growth of the fund industry are mutually-reinforcing trends that drive the marketplace to ever-greater diversity, sophistication, and value. And 401(k) plans are riding that trend full-throttle into the future. For millions of people, it is their best chance for a financially secure retirement. And for tens of thousands of companies, 401(k)s are the retirement plan of choice. If you are looking to buy one, there's never been a better time. With the passage in 2001 of

the Economic Growth and Tax Relief Reconciliation Act (EGTRRA)—
the most significant piece of pension legislation in over a decade—the
opportunity to save and invest has become greater than ever before.[3] (See
the appendix for a summary of the EGTRRA's main provisions.)

GROWTH OF 401(K) ASSETS

The twin engines of 401(k) capital accumulation—tax-deferred
savings and compound growth—are pulling a mighty big train. Consider
these statistics:

+ The total amount of money in those accounts now tops $1.7
  trillion, triple the amount invested ten years ago.[4]
+ Over 45 million American workers are covered by 401(k)
  plans and this number will increase by 6 percent a year,
  reaching nearly 60 million by 2006.[5]
+ The average account balance was $55,000 at year-end 2000.[6]

Let's consider the significance of these numbers. Until recently, the
value of a person's home largely determined an individual's overall
wealth. For many people today, 401(k) represents their single largest
asset and often exceeds the equity in their homes.[7] This means that the
oversight of their retirement money is an important and growing
responsibility. And with so much of their net worth tied up in a 401(k),
you can expect your employees to be watching you closely.

Your employees have the motivation to keep track of their investments
and they have the means to do so. Modern technology allows plan participants to monitor investments as easily as keeping track of the balance
in their checking account. The press churns out article after article telling
401(k) participants what to look for in their plans. Strict federal laws spell
out the rights of plan participants and the responsibilities of plan sponsors. These laws give participants the right to sue. And as the grassroots
movement for greater disclosure and more emphasis on participants'
rights grows, expect more demands and more lawsuits.

For vendors, the future looks bright. Banks, third-party administrators (TPAs), insurance companies, brokerage firms, and mutual fund houses are in fierce competition for a piece of the $1.7 trillion 401(k) pie. And mutual fund companies have already helped themselves to the largest slice.

THE RISE OF THE MUTUAL FUND INDUSTRY

The growth of the mutual fund industry parallels the rise of 401(k) plans and now, mutual funds are the favored funding vehicle for these plans.[8] In the early 1980s, there were less than a thousand mutual funds;[9] today, there are well over twelve thousand.[10]

In 1980, the combined asset base of the mutual fund industry was $100 billion, and had just survived the extended bear market of the early 1970s. Now, flush with nearly $6 trillion of investors' dollars, they seem unbeatable.[11] In the competitive world of mutual fund marketing, the 401(k) marketplace is an arena where a mutual fund company can gain thousands of fund holders overnight, along with tens of millions of assets by taking over a single 401(k) plan. It should be no surprise then that many of the largest mutual fund companies are also the largest 401(k) providers.[12]

For mutual fund companies, 401(k) money flows in like clockwork. The money comes from retirement plans all over the country on bi-weekly or monthly cycles, most of it electronically. Unlike money from individual "retail" investors, which tends to chase performance and move in and out of the hottest funds,[13] most 401(k) investors stay put since they have a long-term investment horizon. This steady pattern allows for predictable cash flows and redemption patterns. Vendors usually make their money from asset-based fees that they charge for investment management. These recurring asset management fees generate considerable revenue. As assets under management increase, so are the fees generated.[14]

✦   ✦   ✦

An Example: Fidelity Investments

Let's look at Fidelity—the largest and best known mutual fund company in the world. It manages over $751.3[15] billion of mutual fund assets representing about 11.7 percent of the entire $5.9 trillion mutual fund industry.[16]

Fidelity achieved its dominant market position in part because they were one of the first companies to make a concerted effort to sell their funds to retirement plans. By packaging its funds inside a bundled 401(k) product and offering them to company-sponsored retirement plans, Fidelity quickly increased its market share. Now slightly more than half of their asset base (56 percent) is considered "retirement."[17]

Here's how they do it. About 80 percent of Fidelity's $78 billion flagship fund, Fidelity Magellan—one of the largest and most popular mutual funds in the country—is made up of retirement plan money like IRAs and 401(k)s.[18] At the time of this writing, Magellan charges .88 percent or 88 basis points[19] of total assets to run the fund. This means that for every $1 million of assets under management, Fidelity generates $8,800. At nearly $80 billion of assets under management, Fidelity grosses $687 million from just this one fund! Small wonder that 401(k) providers are fighting to corral as many plans as possible.

How Mutual Fund Companies Have Transformed the 401(k) Industry

The competition for 401(k) dollars has fueled a buyer's market, and nowhere is this more evident than in the technological transformation of the industry. The mutual fund companies first embraced technology as a way to lure individual retail investors during their go-go growth years of the 1980s. The industry then used what it learned from the retail side to transform the 401(k) market with participant-directed daily valuation technology, quarterly statements, twenty-four-hour toll-free telephone access, and access to call-center reps. These technological advances became possible because of the development of inexpensive yet powerful computers. Before the widespread use of these systems, most first-generation 401(k) plans were valued annually or semi-annually, and plan trustees made investment decisions for all participants.

BUNDLED DELIVERY PLATFORMS

Technological advancements and the push for value in 401(k) plans have resulted in streamlined delivery systems. Mutual fund companies were some of the first to exploit the "bundled" delivery model—tying together core services such as recordkeeping, administration, employee education, compliance, and investments under one roof and dramatically simplifying the lives of sponsors in the process. ("Bundled" is one of those terms that means different things to different people. Basically, if a participant only "sees" one service provider, then the product is bundled.) Today, the bundled delivery platform, an offshoot of the mutual fund revolution in the 401(k) marketplace, has become the dominant service delivery model.[20] This is especially true for companies with less than five hundred employees where during the vendor selection process, emphasis is placed on hassle-free streamlined delivery and low fees.[21]

The primary reasons for "bundling" are simplicity and low cost. All services are delivered by and through a single entity. Bundled providers use asset-based fees to offset recordkeeping costs. This keeps plan sponsor's billed expenses to a minimum, making plans affordable for virtually every company. However, it also makes it harder to figure out just what you're paying for since the costs tend to be buried within the plan. We will discuss this subject later in chapter 11, "Plan Costs."

INVESTMENT ALLIANCES ("SUPERMARKETS") AND THE 401(K) MARKETPLACE

The same powerful computers that allow for participant-directed,[22] daily-valued accounts, and toll-free call-center and Internet access, also permit service providers to string together investment alliances made up of hundreds of retail mutual funds. The investment alliance concept allows sponsors and participants to select investments from a cross-section of mutual fund families through a single recordkeeping platform. This was a radical break from the early 1990s when selecting three to five funds from a single fund family was the norm. Now, because of sophisticated technology and market demand, plan sponsors can routinely pick ten to twenty funds from an investment universe of anywhere from fifty to five thousand funds, depending on the vendor and the size of the plan.

Upshot: It's a Buyer's Market

All of these trends—sophisticated technology, bundled delivery systems and investment alliances—point to the one constant in the 401(k) marketplace: change. Fueling this change is the fierce competition among 401(k) service providers for a share of the 401(k) pie. With the shift in corporate retirement plans from a defined benefit to a defined contribution model, and with the government concerned about future Social Security obligations, individuals are now, more than ever, responsible for their own financial future. Market competition and consumer demand are pushing vendors to provide improved investment options and better tools to monitor retirement accounts. Features that only a few years ago would have been prohibitively expensive for all but the biggest plans, are now commonplace.

So, what does this mean for the person whose job it is to contract a 401(k) plan? First, it's a buyer's market. Whether you are buying for the first time, or are considering replacing your current provider, you can find high-quality plans at reasonable costs. You still have to shop around, ask the tough questions, and negotiate service and performance guarantees. But with so many providers to choose from, you can leverage the competitive fact of the marketplace to get the best deal.

This competition among vendors has led to increased options in 401(k) plans, but it has also increased the pressure on plan sponsors to make the right decisions. With so many vendors, how does one make a good choice? And if you already have a plan, how do you ensure that your selection will stand up to the scrutiny of your employees and your boss? The answer lies in using the right process and following the right steps. This book will guide you through that. But before we begin, let's take a little more time to get our bearings. What exactly is a 401(k)? Why would a company want to set one up in the first place? Are there other kinds of retirement plans to consider? And why do so many employers and employees love 401(k)s?

Notes

1. According to the International Foundation of Employee Benefit Plans, at the end of 2000, there were 377,000 401(k) plans representing $1.7 trillion in assets and 37.1 million participants. *Employee Benefits Digest,* "401(k) Plan Celebrates 20th Anniversary," October 2001, p. 1.

2. The plans are so widespread that they now outnumber traditional pensions four to one, according to benefits trackers at Spectrem Group. The *Augusta Chronicle,* September 7, 2000. Assets in corporate DC plans surpassed corporate DB plan assets. 2000 SPARK Marketplace, p. 2.

3. "Effective January 1, 2002, a nonrefundable tax credit of up to $1,000 is available to certain employees who contribute to their employer's retirement savings program. The credit applies to the first $2,000 of contributions and ranges from 10%–50% of the qualified contributions, depending on the individual's tax filing status and adjusted gross income level. It represents a direct offset against taxes owed." 401(k) Expedition, "New Tax Law Allows Higher Contribution Limits," Mutual of Omaha Companies, December 2001.

    "The new law (i.e., EGTRRA) provides a tax credit for employers with 100 or fewer employees that adopt a retirement plan. The amount of the credit is equal to 50% of the 'qualified start up costs' for the plan, subject to a maximum of $500 per year, for each of the first three years following the adoption of the plan. . . . In addition, the law provides that employers with 100 or fewer employees are exempt from paying the user fees to the IRS for determination letters regarding the qualified status of a pension plan. This exemption applies for the first five years following the adoption of the plan. "Tax Law Makes Numerous Changes to Pension Law," *Retirement Plan Trends,* August 2001, AUL.

4. International Foundation of Employee Benefit Plans, *Employee Benefits Digest,* "401(k) Plan Celebrates 20th Anniversary," October 2001, p. 1.

   The number of people who participated in defined contribution plans reached 62 million as of the end of 2000, and the invested assets of these workers rose to $2.2 trillion. Cerulli Associates Market Update: The 401(k) Industry, 2001.

5. "Retirement Markets in Transition," speech delivered on January 31, 2002 by Cerulli Associates consultant, Scudder Consultant Symposium, Miami, Florida.

6. Depending on who's data you use, there can be a significant difference in average account balances. The most common range today is between $50,000 and $55,000. The following are three different sources for average account balances:

   ✦ "401(k) Plan Asset Allocation, Account Balances, and Loan Activity in 2000," Sarah Holden and Jack VanDerhei, EBRI Issue Brief, November 2001.
   ✦ Investment Company Institute, *2001 Mutual Funds Fact Book,* chapter 5, "Mutual Funds and the Retirement Market," p. 6.
   ✦ Fidelity, *Building Futures:* Volume III, p. 19.

   According to Fidelity, the average account balance in 2000 was $55,000. This book uses the Fidelity numbers.

7. Median home equity for homeowners' households increased between 1991 and 1993 from $43,070 in 1991 to $46,669 in 1993. Median net worth for households in1993 was $37,587. (Asset Ownership of Households: 1993, The Survey of Income and Program Participation (SIPP).)

8. At the end of 2000, mutual funds' share of the 401(k) market was estimated at 45 percent ($766 billion) compared with 9 percent at the beginning of the decade. Investment Company Institute, *2001 Mutual Funds Fact Book,* chapter 5, "Mutual Funds and the Retirement Market," p. 5.

9. 837 funds, Mutual Fund Fact Book, 2000 Edition, Investment Company Institute.

10. Morningstar Principia Pro, December 31, 2001 release.

11. Investment Company Institute, *2001 Mutual Funds Fact Book,* chapter 3, "US Mutual Funds Developments," p. 1.

12. Fidelity, Vanguard, American Funds, Putnam, Janus—"20 Largest Fund Families," Kanon Bloch Carre, December 31, 2000.
Fidelity, Vanguard, CIGNA, Merrill Lynch, Putnam—"Largest 401(k) Defined Contribution Providers." Source: Money Market Directory of Pension Funds and Investment Managers, 2000, based on the number of clients with DC assets of $5 million or more.
   The five largest mutual fund complexes control 34 percent of assets and the top ten control 68 percent. Investment Company Institute, *2001 Mutual Funds Fact Book,* chapter 3, "US Mutual Funds Developments," p. 15.

13. The word "retail" is usually contrasted with the word "institutional," which refers to buyers such as corporate-sponsored retirement plans, endowments, foundations, private trusts, etc.

14. According to Spectrem Group's projections, the aggregate 401(k) marketplace generates $13.204 billion of total fees, of which 89.5 percent ($11.817 billion) is derived from asset fees while the remaining 10.5 percent ($1.387 billion) comes from service fees. "Plan Sponsors Need Better Fix on 401(k) Fees," *Employee Benefit Plan Review,* September 2001, p. 22.

15. Fidelity corporate Web site, December 23, 2001.
http://personal100.fidelity.com/myfidelity/InsideFidelity/index.html

16. *Ibid*

17. *Ibid*

18. *Ibid*

19. A fund's expense ratio is the sum of the various investment management and distribution fees charged by the fund. These fees are broken down in detail in each fund's prospectus.

    According to Magellan's online prospectus:

    + Magellan closed to new investors in 1997.
    + Magellan puts up to 20 basis points of its fee at risk in an unique "performance adjustment" formula. If Magellan outperforms its index, the S&P 500 (calculated monthly based on a rolling 36 months of investment performance), it charges the full fee. If it underperforms relative to the S&P 500, the fee drops.

    http://personal400.fidelity.com/fidbin/getewdoc.cgi?fund=21&doc=frame

20. 75 percent of plan sponsors in 2000 use a full-service platform (bundled and alliance) up from 61 percent in 1996. "Retirement Markets in Transition," speech delivered on January 31, 2002, by Cerulli Associates consultant, Scudder Consultant Symposium, Miami, Florida.

21. Full-service providers include mutual fund companies, larger banks, and insurance companies. In one estimate, there are just over two hundred full-service providers available to plan sponsors (Valletta, February 1997). However, they must control a large segment of the market, since, in a recent survey, it was estimated that 59 percent of 401(k) plans use bundled services from full-service providers (Spencer & Associates). *Money,* December 23, 2001.
    http://401k-administration.com/administration.html

22. Participants direct the investment of 100 percent of their own contributions, the investments of their employer's matching contributions in 80 percent of plans, and profit-sharing contributions in 85 percent of plans according to a survey by William M. Mercer.
    http://www.plansponsor.com/eprise/main/PlanSponsor/News/HR/MercerAssetAlloc

CHAPTER 2

THE RETIREMENT PLAN UNIVERSE

◆

Before we consider 401(k) in detail, it will be useful to understand how it stacks up against other plans within the retirement plan universe. First, we'll look at the terms and categories that define the main types of retirement plans. Then, we'll look at different kinds of plans. Finally, we'll discuss 401(k) in detail and see how it works. Remember, 401(k) is not the only retirement option available, and it's important to determine whether it's the best choice for you. Consider the needs of your company as you weigh the pluses and minuses of the various plans. Understanding the different options available will help you select the right plan for your company.

QUALIFIED VS. NONQUALIFIED PLANS

Let's begin with the big picture. There is a fundamental division in the retirement world between qualified and nonqualified plans. Qualified plans receive preferential tax treatment under the tax code. Money in a qualified plan grows tax-deferred until withdrawal. Employees receive an immediate tax break on their contributions to these plans (i.e., they do not have to pay current state or federal income tax on salary deferrals), and employers receive a deduction for the employees' contributions as well as for the administrative costs of maintaining the plan. In exchange for this privileged tax treatment, qualified plans have to abide by a federal law known as the Employees Retirement Income Security Act of 1974 (ERISA)[1] enforced by three federal agencies: the Internal Revenue Service (IRS), the Department of Labor (DOL),[2] and the Pension Benefit Guaranty Corporation (PBGC)[3].

Nonqualified plans fall outside the scope of government regulations and, by definition, do not have to follow the complex and sometimes cumbersome rules of qualified plans. These plans are usually established for top executives as supplemental retirement plans over and above the qualified plans.

WHY COMPANIES LIKE QUALIFIED PLANS

There are several reasons why companies sponsor qualified retirement plans and why employees like them.

+ Retirement plans improve employee/employer relations and help to attract and retain quality people.[4]
+ Corporate income tax deductions are allowed for company contributions deposited into a plan. In addition, plans often allow for flexibility in determining the amount and timing of employer contributions.
+ Employee contributions are made "pre-tax," i.e., participants do not pay federal or state taxes on the amount contributed.
+ Earnings within the plan (e.g., interest, dividends and capital gains) grow tax-deferred until distributed.
+ Corporate-sponsored retirement plans' contribution limits are higher than limits for Individual Retirement Accounts (IRA).
+ Special tax treatment is available for participants upon distribution. Besides lump-sum distributions, employees may be eligible for multi-year and annuity distribution options.

DEFINED-BENEFIT PLANS

Qualified plans break down into two basic categories: defined-benefit (DB) plans and defined-contribution (DC) plans. DB plans represent a company's "promise to pay" a retirement benefit based on variables such as average income, years of service, and retirement age. For example, $1,000 a month at retirement until death—however long that may be. These plans were popular in the 1950s, 1960s, and 1970s for employees of larger companies and are what most people think of as traditional pension plans; monthly cash benefits that reward long years of service for stable jobs in stable industries. In these highly regulated plans, company contributions are actuarially determined each year on the basis of the benefit formula. With a DB plan, you can calculate today exactly what your benefit will be at the time of your retirement.

If you are currently covered by one of these plans, consider yourself lucky. The company pays for the entire cost of the plan and bears all of the investment risk. If current assets are not sufficient to meet current liabilities, the company must make a contribution to close the gap. Regardless of what happens in the stock market, you are guaranteed your benefit based on the plan's benefit formula.

DB formulas favor older employees who tend to earn more and have more years of service than younger employees. In certain situations, a DB plan can provide a contribution in excess of $150,000 a year on behalf of older employees. This compares to a maximum contribution under a DC plan of $40,000 per year.[5] Although expensive and relatively complex to administer and communicate, a DB plan combined with a DC plan and Social Security give older, longer-term employees an excellent chance of achieving retirement security.

Yet it is precisely this generous design—a typical DB plan is usually worth between 5 and 9 percent of an employee's annual base pay—that makes them expensive to offer. Since these plans are entirely employer-paid, they represent a tremendous value to employees. Unfortunately, they are also shrinking as companies look for ways to control costs and reduce long-term corporate liabilities.[6] Besides cost, the advent of the 401(k) plan, coinciding with increased labor-mobility patterns, additional federal regulations of DB plans, and greater employee understanding of DC than DB plans, influenced a decline in the relative prominence of traditional pension plans in the retirement landscape of American workers. The absolute number of workers covered by DB plans has been in the range of 39 million to 41 million since 1983; however, the growth in the size of the labor force has resulted in a substantial reduction in the percentage of workers covered by DB plans.[7]

DEFINED-CONTRIBUTION PLANS

Unlike with a DB plan, the amount available from a DC plan is not known until retirement. The reason is simple. In a DC plan, a participant's account balance is determined by the level of employer and employee contributions and the investment return over time. The participant bears all of the investment risk in a DC plan. That explains why DC plans favor younger employees: they have more time for tax-deferred compound growth to work. In general, the greater the contribution levels the higher the investment return, and the longer the time period, the higher the participant's retirement benefit. We now turn our attention to the evaluation of specific types of DC plans.

EVALUATING DIFFERENT DEFINED-CONTRIBUTION PLANS

Deciding what type of plan is best suited to your company is crucial. There are several types of DC plans from which to choose, each with its own strengths and weaknesses. The differences between plans can be divided into several broad categories.

- ✦ Contribution limits
- ✦ Contribution flexibility
- ✦ Contribution cost

+ Administrative and regualtory complexity
+ Company growth, demographics, employee expectations, and retirement focus

Below is a brief outline of things to consider as you evaluate different plans. An overview of the main features of each kind of plan follows.

CONTRIBUTION LIMITS

Some plans allow employers to contribute more money than do other plans. If the goal is maximizing retirement savings, DB plans, for example, allow for greater contributions than DC plans for older employees.[8] For a small-business owner who has little or no retirement savings, this may be an attractive option. Even within the DC world, some plans allow for greater contribution limits than others. For example, traditional and Safe Harbor 401(k) plan designs allow participants to set aside $11,000 versus $7,000 in a SIMPLE 401(k).

CONTRIBUTION FLEXIBILITY

Is company cash flow stable or does it fluctuate? Can the company commit to making a fixed contribution every month, quarter, or year, or will it require a plan that does not require fixed employer contributions?

COST OF COMPANY CONTRIBUTIONS

Can the company afford to make contributions? And, if so, how much should it contribute? Should the contribution go to all employees or just to those who will set aside a portion of their salaries as savings? If you work for a public company, should the contribution be in company stock, and, if so, what restrictions, if any, should there be on the employee's ability to transfer the stock?

ADMINISTRATIVE AND REGULATORY COMPLEXITY

Due to varying degrees of government regulations, some plans are more difficult to administer than others. All retirement plans require some degree of employer administration yet some plans require more employer involvement and therefore entail more work than others. If you can't make the necessary commitment, either consider a plan that requires little or no administration, or make sure to hire a vendor with a proven reputation for handling the administrative and regulatory detail of more complex plans. It should be noted, however, that some additional administrative complexity is not necessarily a bad thing, since, generally speaking, it allows for greater plan design flexibility. For example, your ability to exclude part-time employees, attach vesting schedules to employer contributions, or have more control over plan assets, may not be allowed with administratively simple plans.

COMPANY GROWTH

Is the company growing? How long will it be around? The last thing you want to do is start a retirement plan for a company that is going out of business or will soon be sold. Terminating or merging a plan is a complex process that requires time, effort, and money.

COMPANY DEMOGRAPHICS

Is the employee base skewed younger or older? DC plans favor younger employees. Is the wage structure relatively high or low? If it is low, is it realistic to expect employees to be able to save enough on their own for retirement? How many employees do you have? Is turnover high or low? Does the compensation structure fall within a narrow band or are there extremes at either end? Are there a lot of part-time workers and, if so, are you interested in excluding them?

EMPLOYEE EXPECTATIONS

Are you in an industry where traditional pension plans are the norm? For example, an employer that recruits heavily from the Fortune 500 may need a defined-benefit plan to meet employee expectations. For most companies, a retirement plan of some kind is necessary to attract and retain quality employees. Many of today's employees cite the 401(k) plan as the most important benefit after health insurance.[9]

RETIREMENT FOCUS

Whom is the plan intended to benefit? Is the reason for the plan to attract and retain quality employees and to reward them for their hard work, or is it intended to primarily benefit the owners, as is the case with many small companies? As you will see from the following discussion, certain plans can be designed to disproportionately reward the owners and key shareholders of a company.

DEFINED-CONTRIBUTION PLANS: AN OVERVIEW

Defined-contribution plans come in many shapes and sizes. For example, some are specifically designed for companies with less than a hundred employees. One of the following plans should be able to meet your company's needs. (Please see the appendix for a summary table of the main types of DC plans.)

1. SEP and SEP-IRA Plan

In a SEP-IRA, the employer contributes the same percentage to each participant's IRA. This plan is designed for sole proprietors and small businesses, where the employer decides annually what percentage of salary he will contribute up to 25 percent of compensation, or $40,000, whichever is less.[10] If employees choose so, they may combine the company SEP and personal IRA contributions in one account.

The beauty of a SEP plan is in its simplicity and low cost. It does not require an administrator or government filings. And because each participant maintains a separate IRA account, the employer's fiduciary liability is minimized. Unlike a profit-sharing plan, a SEP can exclude from eligibility people with less than three years of employment. Loans are not permitted, and employees are vested immediately upon joining the plan. Part-time employees are eligible for the plan once they meet the three-year eligibility period. A SEP is perfect for employers that don't want the hassle of maintaining a more administratively complex employer-sponsored retirement plan.

2. SIMPLE IRA Plan

"SIMPLE" is an acronym for "Savings Incentive Match Plan for Employees." Introduced by the Small Business Job Protection Act (SBJPA) of 1996, it's targeted at businesses with a hundred or fewer employees. The SIMPLE IRA is designed to offer greater income deferral opportunities than individual retirement accounts (IRAs), with fewer restrictions and administrative requirements than traditional pension or profit-sharing plans.

With this type of plan, an employee can elect to set aside a percentage of his compensation up to $7,000 (excluding employer contributions) in an IRA on a pre-tax basis.[11] Withdrawals prior to age 59 ½ are subject to a 10 percent penalty (25 percent, if the withdrawal is made within the first two years) but earnings grow tax deferred until they are withdrawn at retirement.

Under a qualified salary-reduction arrangement, the employer must make "matching" contributions. That is, the employer must make contributions to an employee's SIMPLE account up to 3 percent of the employee's compensation. For example, if an employee with compensation of $50,000 elects to have 10 percent of his pay contributed to the plan ($5,000), the employer must contribute an additional $1,500 (3 percent of $50,000). If an employer chooses to contribute less than 3 percent, he can give employees proper notice and reduce the contribution to as low as 1 percent of compensation, as long as this isn't done for more than two years out of the five-year period ending with the year of reduced contributions.

Alternatively, instead of making "matching" employee contributions, the employer can simply contribute a flat 2 percent of "compensation" (up to $160,000, as adjusted for inflation) for every eligible employee whether the employee elects to contribute or not. Special notice must be given to employees if the employer wishes to take this approach.[12]

3. Profit-Sharing Plan

The key feature of profit-sharing plans is flexibility. Each year a company decides how much to contribute from 0 to 25 percent of each eligible employee's compensation subject to an annual dollar limit of $40,000.[13] For example, it could contribute 10 percent in year one, 6 percent in year two, and 4 percent in year three. The sponsor can link the contribution to some measure of company performance, such as "profit," but it is not required to.[14] It can even forgo making a contribution if sufficient funds aren't available.[15] A profit-sharing plan makes sense for a company that wants to make annual contributions to employees' accounts, but wants flexibility in deciding the annual contribution.

Profit-Sharing Contribution Formulas

There are four basic different formulas for allocating profit-sharing contributions. These formulas work differently and can be used to reward different groups of employees:

+ **Salary Ratio**—The simplest and by far the most common formula, this formula allocates contributions based on an eligible employee's salary relative to the total eligible salary base. For example, if the company makes a 10 percent contribution, an eligible employee earning $50,000 a year would receive $5,000.

+ **Permitted Disparity**—This contribution formula "integrates" with Social Security, providing a higher benefit to those employees who make more than the Social Security taxable wage base of $84,900 in 2002. For an employee earning $125,000 annually, for example, the employer could contribute 8 percent of an employee's pay ($10,000) plus 5.7 percent above the current wage base ($2,286) for a total of $12,286. The individual earning only $30,000 receives the 8 percent contribution ($2,400) but doesn't receive a contribution under the allocation formula's second tier.

+ **Age-Weighted**—Age-weighted contributions are allocated based on a participant's age (or, more precisely, by a discount factor based on the number of years to normal retirement age) and compensation. This plan allows older and more senior employees who are usually the highest paid group to receive a larger proportion of the company's contributions.

+ **Cross-Tested**[16]—A cross-tested formula allows employers to make contributions based on job designations. It maximizes contributions going to those employees the employer deems to be most vital to a company's success, who may not necessarily be older.[17] "Cross-testing" refers to the process used to satisfy discrimination rules by converting today's contributions into their equivalent benefit accrual rates. Special discrimination testing (sometimes requiring complex actuarial calculations) is required to determine that none of the strict government rules against discrimination have been violated.

Small businesses and professional organizations such as doctor and lawyer groups often use permitted disparity, age-weighted and cross-

tested contribution formulas so as to maximize profit-sharing contributions going to the principals. Although more complex than a simple
"salary ratio" contribution formula, cross-tested plans are generally less
expensive and more flexible than DB plans.

Profit Sharing/401(k) Hybrid

Profit sharing plans can include a 401(k) deferral to form a particularly
powerful design. In this "hybrid" plan, a company makes annual,
discretionary profit-sharing contributions to all eligible employees. In
addition, those employees who want to save more can set aside their
own money on a pre-tax basis in a 401(k). The employer may also
decide to match the employee's 401(k) deferrals. By combining the company's profit-sharing contributions with the employee's 401(k) deferrals
(and possibly a 401(k) matching contribution too), employees stand a
good chance of achieving retirement security.

4. Money Purchase

A money-purchase plan allows a company to deduct up to 25 percent of
aggregate employee compensation subject to an annual limit of $40,000.
Up until 2001, the 25 percent deduction limit of a money-purchase plan
was 10 percent more than the deduction limit of a profit-sharing plan and
was the main reason companies selected a money-purchase design over
profit sharing. The historically higher deduction limit of money-purchase
plans came at a cost; in exchange for the higher limit, a company had to
agree to a fixed contribution percentage. Unlike a profit-sharing contribution that can fluctuate from year to year, a money-purchase contribution
percentage is mandatory and can only be changed by formally amending
the plan. The passage of EGTRRA effectively eliminates the reason for
establishing money-purchase plans since profit-sharing plans now have the
same deduction limit of 25 percent but do not require a mandatory contribution. If you already have a money-purchase plan, you may wish to
merge it into your profit-sharing/401(k) plan. By doing so, you'll eliminate
the need for filing two separate Form 5500s and possibly lower the costs
associated with maintaining two separate plans.

5. Target Benefit

A target-benefit plan combines many features of a DB plan, yet at its core it remains a DC plan. As in a DB plan, the employer's contributions are calculated yearly on the basis of a participant's salary, years of service, and other actuarial assumptions. Unlike a DB plan, however, the participant assumes 100 percent of the investment risk, and the retirement balance is not known in advance but is determined by the participant's investment selections and their performance. The maximum contribution limitation is 25 percent. Because they use a funding formula, which weights salary and years of service, target-benefit plans favor older, more highly paid employees. A target-benefit plan makes sense for a company that is willing and able to make annual recurring contributions and wants to favor older, higher paid employees.

6. 403(b)

These plans are only available to non-profit organizations.[18] Employees can contribute up to $11,000 per year on a tax-deferred basis and, beginning in 2002, "catch up" contributions are allowed.[19] Just like with a 401(k), an employer can match a portion of participants' contributions to a 403(b) plan. Due to legislative tinkering, 401(k) and 403(b) plans are converging with respect to plan design. One major difference remains, however; 403(b) plans do not have to conduct annual discrimination testing of the kind required by 401(k) plans—a topic we discuss in detail in chapter 4. The other meaningful difference lies in the competitive nature of the service provider marketplace; generally speaking, the 401(k) marketplace is larger and more competitive than the 403(b) marketplace.

7. 457(b) Plans

Section 457 of the IRS Code allows certain governmental organizations to sponsor a plan whereby employees can defer up to $11,000 on a pre-tax basis for retirement. The types of organizations include state, city, township, state agency or political subdivision such as a school district, and any organization exempt from federal income tax (including non-profits) except for a church or synagogue. Beginning in 2002, "catch up" contributions like those found in 401(k) and 403(b) plans are allowed. In addition, 457 plans can be offered to selected employees as non-discrimination testing is not required of these plans. In an interesting twist, non-profits may wish to add a 457(b) plan to their existing 403(b) or 401(k) plan since an employee participating in both would be able to defer $22,000; $11,000 in a 401(k) or 403(b) and another $11,000 in a 457(b).[20]

8. Traditional 401(k)

401(k) is a special kind of profit-sharing plan and the only non-IRA qualified plan that allows employees to defer a portion of their own money (up to 100 percent of earned income or an annual dollar limit of $11,000, whichever is less) on a pre-tax basis. (With the passage of EGTRRA, individuals aged 50 or older are allowed to make special "catch up" contributions.) Although most companies make some kind of matching contribution, it is also the only corporate retirement plan that does *not* require an employer contribution, thus making the sponsor's cost potentially zero. This fact helps explain the amazing popularity and growth of the 401(k). As I mentioned earlier, a 401(k) plan can also include an employer-paid profit-sharing contribution to form a particularly powerful plan design. Because of its low-cost and flexible nature, for many companies, especially small ones, the choice is often 401(k) or nothing.

Two Variations on 401(k)

A 401(k) must pass annual discrimination tests to ensure compliance with IRS regulations, a subject we will discuss in chapter 4. Depending on the results of these tests, Highly Compensated Employees (HCEs)[21] may be required to return some or all of their pre-tax deferrals, or the company may be required to make additional contributions to Non–Highly Compensated Employees (NHCEs). Congress recently created two variations on the traditional 401(k) plan that allow sponsors to bypass annual testing requirements as long as the employer makes certain minimum contributions . By adopting one of these plan designs, HCEs can make maximum contributions without fear of jeopardizing the plan's ability to pass the tests. Let's look at these special 401(k) plan designs in more detail.

- ✦ **SIMPLE 401(k)**—This option is for companies with less than a hundred eligible employees who have no other qualified retirement plans. If a company makes either an immediately vested dollar-for-dollar matching contribution of up to 3 percent of salary to all 401(k) participants or a 2-percent contribution to all eligible employees (regardless of whether they participate or not), the plan is not subject to annual discrimination testing.[22] A drawback is that in exchange for simplified compliance reporting, the maximum deferral amount is $7,000, compared to $11,000 in a traditional 401(k).

- ✦ **Safe Harbor 401(k)**—Any size company may consider this option.[23] There are two contribution alternatives a company can consider for Safe Harbor 401(k). The plan can make an immediately vested 3-percent contribution to all NHCEs who are eligible to participate in the 401(k) plan. Alternatively, the employer may elect to make immediately vested matching contributions to NHCEs equal to 100 percent of the first 3 percent of employee contributions, plus 50 percent of the next 2 percent of employee contributions.[24]

Why Employees Love 401(k)s

Like most good things, a 401(k) is simple. An employee can elect to set aside $11,000 per year, or 100 percent of her salary, whichever is less. The employee does not pay taxes on the money going into the plan, and the money grows tax-deferred until retirement.[25] The maximum annual contribution including employee deferrals, company-matching and profit-sharing contributions (if applicable), and "forfeitures"[26] is

$40,000. For most Americans, a 401(k) plan is the most efficient way to save for retirement since employees can salt away far more money in a 401(k) than in an IRA.[27] With pre-tax contributions and tax-deferred growth, it's easy to see why employees love them, especially when the employer makes a matching contribution. For many Americans, the investment options offered through their 401(k) may be their last best chance at achieving retirement security.

Why Companies Love 401(k) Plans

401(k) plans are part of a company's benefits package. Smart companies use benefits to attract and retain quality employees in order to be more competitive. 401(k) plans represent value to a company because of their high visibility and low cost. Compared to health insurance, where in any given year a small percentage of the employees incur the majority of claims, virtually everyone shares the rewards of a retirement benefit. And as mentioned before, although most employers make some kind of matching contribution, it is not required. Administrative costs can be paid for entirely by the employer, by the employee, or, as is most often the case, shared. Most employees are aware of 401(k) plans and cite them as the second most important benefit after health insurance. Finally, just like any other employee benefit, the costs associated with the plan are considered tax-deductible business expenses.[28]

The first step in making a good buying decision is to understand the fundamental legal and regulatory underpinnings of 401(k) plans, the subject of the next three chapters.

Notes

1. Enacted in 1974, ERISA (29 U.S.C.S. §1001 et seq.) governs the conduct of employers who sponsor qualified retirement plans and health and welfare benefit plans. ERISA imposes fiduciary duties of loyalty, prudence and prudent diversification of plan assets upon employers who sponsor retirement plans.

2. "The U.S. Department of Labor is responsible . . . for the administration and

enforcement of over 180 federal statutes. These legislative mandates and the regulations produced to implement them cover a wide variety of workplace activities . . . including protecting workers' wages, health and safety, employment and pension rights." *http://www.dol.gov/opa/aboutdol/mission.htm*

3. The Pension Benefit Guaranty Corporation (PBGC) protects the retirement incomes of more than 43 million American workers—one of every four working persons—in nearly 38,000 private defined benefit pension plans. *http://www.pbgc.gov/about/default.htm*

4. "Small employers that sponsor a retirement plan say that offering the plan has a positive impact on both their ability to attract and retain quality employees and the attitude and performance of those employees. Furthermore, small employers that offer retirement plans tend to have higher revenues than those that do not sponsor retirement plans." These were among the findings of The 2001 Small Employer Retirement Survey, conducted by the Employee Benefit Research Institute, the American Savings Education Council, and a market research firm."
"Retirement Plan Helps Small Companies Recruit Employees, Earn Revenues," *Retirement Plan Trends,* August 2001, AUL.

"Seventy-eight percent of full-time and part-time workers believe the benefits package that a prospective employer offers is important in their decision to accept or reject a job offer." EBRI Retirement Income Research: 2000 Findings, *www.ebri.org.*

5. The maximum annual benefit that may be funded in a DB plan is generally the lesser of (1) 100 percent of the high three-year average of compensation or (2) $160,000. Tax Law 2001: Pension and Benefits, AIM funds, p. 1–2. IRC §415(b)(1)(A).

6. In 1975, there were 103,000 DB plans. At the end of 1997, there were 53,000. International Foundation of Employee Benefit Plans, *Employee Benefits Digest,* "401(k) Plan Celebrates 20th Anniversary," October 2001, p. 4.

7. EBRI Issue Brief 190. The percentage of full-time workers covered by DB plans in medium and large firms declined from 63 percent in 1988 to 54 percent in 1995

(Bureau of Labor Statistics, July 1997). Further, the number of firms offering DB plans has shrunk, and the incidence of DB plans in small and medium firms is low. *http://www.401(k)helpcenter.com/401(k)_defined.html* (February 19, 2001).

8. See note 5, page 35.

9. "Survey on Employee Savings Plans: 2000–2001," William M. Mercer, p. 1.

10. *http://advisorexpress.fidelity.com/cgi-bin/client*

11. $7,000 in 2002, $8,000 in 2003, $9,000 in 2004, $10,000 in 2005 and then subject to cost-of-living adjustments in $500 increments. Individuals aged 50 or older will also be allowed to make additional "catch up" contributions of $500 in 2002, $1,000 in 2003, $1,500 in 2004, $2,000 in 2005, and $2,500 in 2006. Diversified Investment Advisors, "Economic Growth and Tax Relief Reconciliation Act of 2001 (EGTRRA)," p. 2.

12. *http://www.rudlercpa.com/taxplanning/pension/simple.asp*

13. Until 2001, the maximum corporate deduction for a profit-sharing plan was 15 percent of aggregate compensation paid to eligible employees. With EGTRRA, that percentage increased to 25 percent. Diversified Investment Advisors, "Economic Growth and Tax Relief Reconciliation Act of 2001 (EGTRRA)," p. 2.

14. Since 1986, company profit-sharing contributions are not tied to corporate profitability.

15. While an employer maintaining a discretionary profit-sharing plan is not required to make a contribution every year, there must be "recurring and substantial contributions out of profits for the employees" as indicia that the plan was intended to satisfy the permanency requirement under Treas. Reg. Sec. 1.401-1(b)(2).

16. These plans are also referred to as "comparability" or "new comparability" plans.

17. "Cross-testing allows a more even distribution of the employer allocation than age weighted allocations. This is of particular benefit to employers who are unwilling or

unable to adopt an age-weighted plan because the age differences among employees who are at the same pay but different ages produce uneven allocations between employees."

http://www.eerisa.com/understandingplans/whyaplan/plandesigns.html

18. 403(b) plans are quite similar to 401(k) plans. The biggest remaining difference is that traditional 401(k) plans are required to conduct annual discrimination tests (ADP/ACP), and 403(b) plans are not. Although nonprofit entities may implement a 401(k) plan, corporations are not allowed to start a 403(b) plan.

19. For 401(k), 403(b), and 457(b) plans, the maximum contribution is $11,000 in 2002, $12,000 in 2003, $13,000 in 2004, $14,000 in 2005, and $15,000 in 2006. Individuals aged 50 or older will also be allowed to make additional "catch up" contributions of $1,000 in 2002, $2,000 in 2003, $3,000 in 2004, $4,000 in 2005, and $5,000 in 2006. Diversified Investment Advisors, "Economic Growth and Tax Relief Reconciliation Act of 2001 (EGTRRA)," p. 2.

    The Maximum Exclusion allowance (MEA) were complex and cumbersome calculations that allowed 403(b) participants to make catch up contributions. Due to the passage of EGTRRA, they have been repealed, and simpler, standardized catch-up provisions have replaced them.

20. "457 + 401 = Opportunities", Donald Jay Korn, *Financial Planning,* February 2002.

21. Highly Compensated Employees, or HCEs, are those earning more than $90,000 a year, as adjusted.

22. The salary deferral limit of SIMPLE IRAs and SIMPLE 401(k)s is $7,000 in 2002, $8,000 in 2003, $9,000 in 2004, $10,000 in 2005, and then subject to cost-of-living adjustments each year in $500 increments. Individuals aged 50 or older will also be allowed to make additional "catch up" contributions of $1,000 in 2002, $2,000 in 2003, $3,000 in 2004, $4,000 in 2005, and $5,000 in 2006. Diversified Investment Advisors, "Economic Growth and Tax Relief Reconciliation Act of 2001 (EGTRRA)," p. 2.

23. If you already sponsor a 401(k) plan and wish to convert to "safe harbor" status, you

must do it in conjunction with your plan year. When a 401(k) plan is on a calendar year, the plan can not be converted from a non-safe harbor 401(k) plan to a safe harbor 401(k) plan until the beginning of a new plan year. This means that if a plan is on a calendar year, the plan can commence as a safe harbor plan on January 1, 20xx, but not in the middle (for example) of the prior plan year. When a plan is converted from a non-safe harbor to a safe harbor plan, appropriate notice must be sent to the participants no earlier than 30 and no later than 90 days before the end of the new plan year. In contrast to the rules regarding converting *to* a safe harbor plan, if a plan already operates as a safe harbor 401(k) plan it can convert to a non-safe harbor plan in the middle of a plan year, and is not required to wait until the beginning of the next plan year.

24. There is also a safe harbor for the matching contributions, which, if satisfied, would eliminate the need to test matching contributions. In order to satisfy the requirements for the safe harbor, (1) the employer must not match deferrals which exceed 6 percent of the employee's compensation; (2) the rate of match must not increase as deferrals increase (i.e. you cannot have a formula such as 50 percent up to 3 percent and 100 percent of the next 3 percent); and (3) matching contributions cannot be available to HCEs at a higher rate than are available to Non Highly Compensated Employees at any rate of deferral. *http://www.iraexpert.com/articles/401(k)safe.htm*

25. The IRS has released new guidance on age 70½ distributions from qualified plans (other than certain church and government plans) and section 403(b) tax-sheltered annuities. The guidance was necessary because of changes to the minimum distribution requirements enacted by the 1996 Small Business Job Protection Act (SBJPA). Before these changes, plans had to start paying minimum distributions to participants at age 70½, even if they had not retired. The SBJPA amended Code section 401(a)(9) so that as of January 1, 1997, most employees must begin receiving minimum distributions by April 1 of the calendar year following the *later* of:

(1) the calendar year in which they turn age 70½, or
(2) the calendar year in which they retire.

Five percent owners of the employer must begin receiving minimum distributions by April 1 following the calendar year in which they turn age 70½.

26. Forfeiture money is "unvested" money returned back to the plan. Depending on how the plan is written, forfeitures can be distributed to remaining participants or used to reduce current/future employer contributions.

27. $11,000 versus $3,000. "Catch up" contributions for employees 50 or older allow for even greater savings.

28. ". . . the law provides a three-year tax credit for expenses incurred by employers with 100 or fewer employees in connection with the adoption of a retirement plan. The amount of the tax credit is equal to 50% of the ordinary and necessary expenses paid in connection with the establishment or administration of the plan, subject to a maximum of $500 per year." "Recent Law Changes Make Adopting a Pension Plan Even More Advantageous," *Retirement Plan Trends,* December 2002, AUL.

CHAPTER 3

FIDUCIARY RESPONSIBILITY

Imagine for a moment that you are in the process of building your own home. You've worked with an architect, and a multitude of contractors for plumbing, electricity, masonry, heating and ventilation, millwork, interior design, landscaping, and painting. Or maybe you've just hired one builder to do it all for you—a general contractor to take it from start to finish. In either case, after the house is finished, after you've moved in, if something goes wrong, you'll have someone to blame. You can point to the plumber if the pipes leak, the landscaper if the shrubs die. You can take all of your complaints to the general contractor, if that's the person who's responsible.

Now, consider the process of buying a 401(k). If you are a fiduciary, you are not only the architect, you are also the builder, the structural engineer, the plumber, the painter, and the landscaper. If anything goes amiss—if a disgruntled employee decides to sue because his retirement account hasn't grown quickly enough—you're it. You're liable. "But wait," you say, "I used subcontractors," "I outsourced the buying process, the plan administration, the investment monitoring," and so you did, but you're still responsible.[1] And under the law, ignorance is no excuse.

If the bricks on your new house start to crumble a few months after

40

you move in and you discover that the mason used an inferior variety of brick, no one would argue that you should have understood the chemistry of brick making and that it's your fault. You were swindled. However, if you buy an inferior 401(k) product—a plan with excessive fees, inferior recordkeeping and sub-optimum investment performance—the law says that you should have understood the fine points of the plan, the construction, the chemistry of 401(k). It's your fault.

As account balances grow and as the financial implications of a plan sponsor's poor buying decision become clear, participant lawsuits will likely increase. This is easy to understand. A participant with $4,000 in her 401(k) account might not be willing to sue over issues of investment choice, lack of proper investment education, bungled recordkeeping, or excessive plan costs. But when $400,000 is on the line, she will. The motivation to sue surges when the amount in question represents a participant's financial security.

Retirement looms just over the horizon for millions of baby boomers, and with it, the realization for many that their retirement funds are not what they expected them to be. The spectacular crash of the high-flying dot-coms and the end of the great bull market of the 1990s has already affected millions of 401(k) participants[2]. The consensus among pension experts is that in the next two decades, there will be monumental litigation.[3] As a fiduciary, you must make sure that you are protected from a participant's line of fire. Remember, under the law, ignorance is no excuse. You must follow a specified process and document that process. You must be able to prove that you employed "procedural due diligence." This is a theme I will return to again and again in this book. It cannot be emphasized enough.

In this chapter, we will discuss the specific duties of fiduciaries and look at ways to minimize fiduciary liability. Keep in mind, however, that "minimize" does not mean "eliminate." There is no way to completely avoid liability. As I said earlier, even if you outsource parts of the buying process and plan implementation, you are still responsible for picking the right help. In chapter 13, "Putting It All Together—Vendor Selection," we will discuss how best to hire outside help. For now, though, let's concentrate on your fiduciary responsibilities.

ERISA AND FIDUCIARY RESPONSIBILITY

First, the basics. All qualified retirement plans are governed by ERISA, or the Employee Retirement Income Security Act. Passed in 1974, and enforced by the Department of Labor, it was designed to protect the interests of employee benefit plan participants, including retirement plan participants. ERISA regulates employee eligibility, vesting, minimum funding requirements, administration of plans and plan assets, and disclosure and reporting of plan information to participants and beneficiaries. It also outlines fiduciary responsibilities and strict standards of behavior. ERISA is serious business: a federal law with federal penalties, some of which include personal liability for fiduciaries.[4]

Two government agencies, the Department of Labor (DOL) and the Internal Revenue Service (IRS), are interested in fiduciary conduct. The DOL is charged with monitoring the operation of employee-benefit plans and protecting the rights of retirement plan participants and beneficiaries. The DOL's primary focus is on whether fiduciary actions demonstrate "skill," "prudence," or "loyalty." The IRS, on the other hand, is focused on compliant plan documentation and operation.

FIDUCIARIES

Who is a fiduciary? The government's definition is someone who falls into one of the categories below:

- ✦ Exercises any discretionary authority or control over the management of the plan or the disposition of its assets
- ✦ Offers investment advice regarding plan assets and derives compensation for it—either direct or indirect
- ✦ Has any discretionary authority or responsibility regarding plan administration[5]

Fiduciaries can include a spectrum of people. If a person, or a group of people, exercises any control over a plan, over the management of the plan, or over the investment of plan assets, the definition of "fiduciary" will generally be met. Therefore, as a practical matter, a plan's fiduciaries usually include the plan administrator, all members of a plan's administrative committee, the investment manager and any investment consultant or broker on whose advice the plan relies. Typically, though, for most plans, the fiduciaries are the sponsor, the trustee, and the plan administrator.

As a fiduciary, you are required to act in the best interests of the plan and its participants. By setting up a plan, a fiduciary accepts the responsibilities outlined in ERISA and fiduciary actions, are held to very high standards. Failure to comply could lead to a breach of duty and expose the fiduciary to lawsuits by participants and possible civil and criminal penalties by the Department of Labor.

Duties of a Fiduciary

As a steward of other people's money, a fiduciary has serious responsibilities. The fiduciary is held to a high standard—that of a "prudent man" in matters pertaining to the pension plan. *Merriam-Webster's Dictionary* defines "prudent" as "using good judgement or common sense in handling practical matters." Section 404(a)(1)(B) of ERISA requires that:

> "A fiduciary shall discharge his duties . . . with the care, skill, prudence, and diligence, under the circumstances then prevailing that a prudent man acting in a like capacity and familiar with such matters would use in the conduct of an enterprise of a like character and with like aims."[6]

In matters of such importance, you are expected to know your responsibilities and to execute them in good faith with the best interests of the participants in mind. Lack of knowledge is no excuse even when hiring independent advisors. If you hire someone who gives you bad advice, you could still be held liable if you cannot prove due diligence in the hiring process.

Fiduciary responsibilities can be split into two main areas: administration and investment management. Here, then, is a list of the basic duties of a fiduciary under ERISA.

Administration[7]

+ Establish the plan in accordance with a written plan document.
+ Operate the plan according to the terms of the written plan document.
+ Act in the exclusive interest of participants and control the expenses of administration.
+ Ensure that the plan is in compliance with all legal and regulatory requirements.
+ Use care to prevent others from committing breaches.
+ Hold plan assets within the jurisdiction of U.S. Courts.
+ Be bonded in the amount of 10 percent of plan assets up to a maximum of $500,000.
+ Do not engage in prohibited transactions.

Investments

+ Make decisions with a level of care that a person familiar with retirement plans would use under the same circumstances.
+ Monitor investment performance.
+ Diversify investments to minimize risk.

By following these regulations closely, you will ensure that your plan is in compliance. Let's take a closer look at some of the most misunderstood of these duties.

1. *Act in the exclusive interest of participants and control the expenses of administration*

A fiduciary is required to act in the best interests of the participants, not the company, and to defray reasonable expenses of administering the plan. The last point—defraying reasonable expenses—

makes two assumptions: (1) the fiduciary knows what the total plan costs are; (2) the fiduciary knows what is "reasonable."

Of course, plan sponsors know what the costs are, right? Wrong! The fact is, most plan sponsors do not know all the costs of their plan and thus cannot judge what constitutes a "reasonable" expense. In the often confusing and convoluted world of 401(k) pricing, many vendors do not take the time to explain how their pricing works, and many sponsors don't bother to ask. Only a handful of vendors routinely explain how their pricing stacks up against national data. And yet as hard as it is to believe, fiduciaries routinely entrust their multimillion dollar 401(k) plans to providers without understanding the fees built into the plan. Unfortunately, this is not a case of "what you don't know won't hurt you." For fiduciaries in the dark about pricing, the implications are serious.

Plan participants are usually the ones who pay the fees and, as a result, end up with smaller retirement balances. And, when these participants realize the extent to which their retirement savings have been compromised by higher-than-necessary fees, someone is going to have to answer. That someone is the fiduciary. We will discuss 401(k) pricing in much more detail in chapter 11, "Plan Costs."

2. Make decisions with a level of care that a person familiar with retirement plans would use under the same circumstances.

The second fiduciary provision says that the decisions you make about the plan will be held to the "Prudent Man" standard. It isn't enough to try your best to make the right decisions. You must use the same decision-making criteria as someone who is an expert in the field. This means that unless you are thoroughly versed in all aspects of retirement plans, it is incumbent upon you to hire qualified experts to help you through the process. We will discuss the pros and cons of third-party professionals in chapter 13, "Putting It All Together—Vendor Selection."

3 (& 4). Monitor investment performance and diversify invest-
ments to minimize risk.

The third and fourth duties, regarding diversification and monitoring of investments, strongly imply the need for formal investment criteria, or a written Investment Policy Statement (IPS), to
guide the fiduciaries in the evaluation, selection, and monitoring
of investments. The responsibility here lies with process and procedure rather than return on investment or selecting from a list of
"best" funds. An IPS is a blueprint or map, created by the plan
sponsor to determine which investments are appropriate for the
plan. A thorough IPS specifies the investment objectives of the
plan and the way investments are selected and monitored. A good
IPS will take into consideration the nature of the company, the
number and kind of investments, and will cover in detail the
investment selection and ongoing monitoring criteria. We will
discuss the role of an investment policy and ways of constructing
one in chapter 9, "Investments."

Minimizing Fiduciary Liability

Fiduciaries can take steps to minimize their exposure to fiduciary liability.
The following steps (broken down into procedural and 404(c)) are
designed to avoid litigation, but in the event of a lawsuit, following these
measures should increase the chance of a quick and favorable outcome.

Procedural

+ First, make sure that everyone involved in the decision-making
  process understands his responsibilities as described in ERISA.
  This means that participants' interests come first. Familiarity
  with fiduciary responsibilities as defined in ERISA is essential,
  since it provides the language of proper conduct.

+ Second, make sure that the plan is administered according to the
  terms of the plan. This requires that all necessary documents

(e.g., Plan Document, Summary Plan Description, Adoption Agreement, Trust Agreement, etc.) be kept up to date, on file, and easily accessible. A periodic review of administrative procedures also makes sense. If a compliance audit discovers that certain procedures have not been followed correctly, call an ERISA attorney immediately to determine an appropriate course of action.

✦ Third, document each significant plan decision. You should leave a paper trail describing why a decision was made and how it was in the best interests of the participants. Operate under the assumption that some day your decisions and actions will be called into question. Proper documentation, showing that an action is consistent with plan documents and in the best interests of participants, is at the heart of procedural due diligence. Process, not outcome, demonstrates fiduciary duty. With no written records, no "paper trail," it is difficult to demonstrate procedural diligence.

✦ Fourth, avoid all real or perceived conflicts of interest. It's not worth jeopardizing the integrity of the plan for some kind of short-term gain.

✦ Fifth, conduct regular audits of the plan. Companies with more than a hundred eligible employees, which offer a 401(k) plan, are required to conduct an annual audit—a service usually handled by the firm's external auditors. A thorough audit ensures that all necessary plan documents exist, are signed, and are in compliance. Basic administrative procedures (e.g., loans, distributions, QDROs, etc.) and forms (e.g., elective deferrals, withholdings, etc.) should be reviewed for compliance and accuracy. Plan operations, such as eligibility and service, spousal consent, hardship distributions, and timely deposit of employee deferrals, should be randomly sampled to ensure accuracy. A review of all necessary compliance testing and government filings is also recommended.

✦ Finally, in addition to the fidelity bond required by ERISA, buy fiduciary liability insurance.[8] Remember, as a fiduciary, you can be held personally liable. In a litigious age, it makes sense to minimize your exposure.

Plan sponsors and fiduciaries can also reduce their liability by taking advantage of relief provided by the Department of Labor through 404(c) regulations.

DOL 404(c) Guidelines

In 1992, the Department of Labor issued final regulations designed to provide limited fiduciary relief to plan sponsors in participant investment–directed plans. Specifically, in a 404(c) compliant plan, the sponsor is not liable for investment losses resulting from the participant's control. In order to satisfy 404(c) requirements, the regulations state that the plan must meet the following three conditions:

+ Offer at least three materially different and internally diversified core investment options, such as a money market, bond, and stock options.
+ Allow for investment exchanges to occur at least quarterly (and more frequently if the volatility of the investments requires it).
+ Provide sufficient information about all investment options, so participants can make informed investment decisions. These include general objectives, historical returns, top security holdings, fees, etc. For plans that use registered investments, i.e., mutual funds, this information is contained in the prospectus.

In addition to the above, plan sponsors must also disclose to participants that the plan voluntarily complies with ERISA Section 404(c) and, therefore, that the plan fiduciaries may be relieved of liability for any losses resulting from a participant's investment decisions. This can be disclosed in the summary plan description (SPD) or in a separate notice. The following additional information must also be disclosed:

+ A description of investment options
+ The identity of investment managers
+ Investment instructions and restrictions
+ Transaction fees
+ The name of the plan fiduciary responsible for providing information
+ Prospectuses
+ "Pass-through" proxy materials

With plan sponsors increasingly seeking its protection, 404(c) compliance is like an insurance policy. Most plans need only to continue their current practices to comply (the "premium"), yet it does provide relief by transferring the liability of investment decisions squarely on participant shoulders (the "protection"). It is worth noting, however, that 404(c) regulations clearly state that the plan fiduciaries are still responsible for the selection and monitoring of the investment options since this liability cannot be transferred.[9]

In its Interpretive Bulletin 96-1, "Participant Investment Education," published in June 1996, the DOL also clarified that general investment education could be provided to participants without risk of fiduciary liability. The Bulletin gives many examples but generally speaking, as long as a sponsor provides objective education materials (e.g., plan information, general investment, asset allocation models and interactive investment materials, etc.) and does not recommend specific investment options, she is not assuming the responsibility (and liability) for participants' investment decisions.[10] We will be discussing employee education strategies for reducing liability in chapter 10, "Employee Communication, Education, and Investment Advice."

Built into the 401(k) legal framework are serious responsibilities for fiduciaries who, as we said, are "it" if something goes wrong. There are ways to minimize fiduciary responsibility, but there's no way to avoid it entirely. If you are a fiduciary, the law demands that you discharge your duties with "skill, prudence, and diligence." In the next chapter, "401(k) Compliance Tests," we look at the rules that make up the framework of every 401(k). As a fiduciary-designer-builder, you'll need a clear understanding of how 401(k)s are put together from the ground up.

Notes

1. "To the extent a plan fiduciary can, and does, delegate his fiduciary duties to others, he relieves himself of nothing but detail. He retains the responsibility to monitor and review the performance of those to whom the duties have been delegated." "Fiduciary Liability: A Perspective for the 1990s," *Kwasha Lipton Newsletter,* v. 24, no. 1, May 1992, p. 2.

   ERISA requires fiduciaries to discharge their duties with respect to a plan "solely in the interest of the participants and beneficiaries.. . . with the care, skill, prudence, and diligence under the circumstances . . . that a prudent man . . . would use . . . ." See ERISA §404(a)(1)(B).

   Moreover, ERISA can hold a fiduciary liable for the breach of fiduciary responsibility of another fiduciary with respect to the same plan. See ERISA §405. This means, as courts have consistently ruled, that a fiduciary has some duty to monitor the activities of other fiduciaries. For example, the court in *Martin v. Harline,* 15 Emp. Ben. Cas. (BNA) 1138 (D Utah 1992), held that the failure to use prudence in appointing a fiduciary and the subsequent failure by the appointing fiduciary "to monitor the fiduciary's performance of his duties" exposes an appointing fiduciary to liability.

2. "Thirteen percent of investors polled recently said that they would have to delay retirement because of stock losses. . . . More than 22% of the respondents in the 55-64 age group said they would have to work longer. The proportion rose to one-fourth for those 65 and older." "Retirements Delayed by Losses, Survey Says," *New York Times,* February 17, 2002, Business Section, p.8.

3. Problems with the trustee system have been around for years, though the number of fiduciary-breach cases brought by the Labor Department has remained relatively steady in recent years, totalling 2,500 cases for the fiscal year ended Sept. 30, 2001,

mostly against small plans. But the number of cases involving 401(k) plans has increased, possibly as employer-sponsors become delinquent in plan payments amid the recent economic downturn, says Ann Combs, the Labor Department's assistant secretary for pension- and welfare-benefits administration.

The difference now is that plan participants at larger companies are complaining more, as the stockmarket slump has sent the value of some plans plunging. As more high-profile accounting scandals come to light, from Enron to Global Crossing to Rite Aid, lawyers are expanding the focus of lawsuits from company directors and executives to pension-plan trustees.

"Fiduciary Breach Cases on the Rise," Kathy Chen, *The Wall Street Journal, www.msnbc.com/news/758666.asp*

4. As set forth in ERISA, §409(a), "(a)ny person who is a fiduciary with respect to a plan who breaches any of the responsibilities, obligations, or duties imposed upon fiduciaries by this title shall be personally liable to make good to such plan any losses to the plan resulting from each such breach, and to restore to such plan any profits of such fiduciary which have been made through use of assets of the plan by the fiduciary and shall be subject to such other equitable or remedial relief as the court may deem appropriate, including removal of such fiduciary."

5. "Generally speaking, any person who exercises discretion or authority with respect to the control or maintenance of employee benefit plan assets will be deemed a fiduciary under ERISA section 3(21). Therefore, the definition of fiduciary under ERISA includes any person who performs any of the following:

- ✦ Exercises any discretionary authority or control over the management of the plan generally or with respect to the management or disposition of plan assets.
- ✦ Renders investment advice with respect to plan assets for a fee or other compensation.
- ✦ Excercises any discretionary authority or responsibility in the plan's administration.

Deciding whether a person has any authority just described is a factual question, demanding an examination of the facts and circumstances of each case. Formal titles

are not controlling. Thus a person's status as a fiduciary depends on his or her function, authority, and responsibility regardless of that person's own belief about whether he or she is a fiduciary."
"The 401(k) Plan Management Handbook," Jeffrey Miller and Maureen Phillips, Irwin Professional Publishing, 1996, p. 149

6. ERISA requires fiduciaries to discharge their duties with respect to a plan "solely in the interest of the participants and beneficiaries. . . . with the care, skill, prudence, and diligence under the circumstances . . . that a prudent man . . . would use. . . ." See ERISA §404(a)(1)(B).

7. ERISA §§ 402(a)(1); 404(a)(1)(A)(i); 404(a)(1)(A)(ii); 404(a)(1)(C); 404(b); 405(a); 405(b); 406(a); 406(b); 406(c); 412.

8. With lawsuits such as First Union's in mind, employers are giving more thought to beefing up trustee education, in hopes of protecting themselves from lawsuits, and are buying more liability insurance. John Coonan, a vice president at Chubb & Son, an insurer, says Chubb received 40% more requests from brokers to underwrite fiduciary-liability insurance for new customers for the first quarter from the year-earlier period.
"Fiduciary Breach Cases on the Rise," Kathy Chen, *The Wall Street Journal,* *www.msnbc.com/news/758666.asp*

9. Regulatory & Legislative Brief, v. XXVI, Winter 1998, Fidelity Institutional Retirement Services Company.

10. ERISA Section 404(c): Shifting Fiduciary Liability in Participant-Directed Retirement Plans, Pension & Benefits Weekly, January 12, 1998.

CHAPTER 4

401(K) COMPLIANCE TESTS

There are a myriad of laws governing 401(k)s. Fortunately you don't have to understand all of them to start or operate a plan. For now, our attention is on the rules and regulations that define the basic framework. We will look at what 401(k)s are made of and how they are put together. As you will see, a 401(k) plan requires a solid bit of work.

STRUCTURE COMMON TO ALL QUALIFIED PLANS

Federal law spells out guidelines, which every qualified retirement plan must meet in order to maintain its tax-advantaged, "qualified" status. The requirements listed below are from Section §401 of the Internal Revenue Code.[1]

+ The plan must be in writing.
+ The plan must be communicated.
+ The assets must be in trust.
+ The plan must be permanent and continuing.
+ The plan assets must be used exclusively for employees.
+ The plan cannot discriminate.

All qualified plan assets are held in trust—a separate legal entity which keeps the assets of the company separate from the assets of the plan.[2] Plan trustees provide oversight to the plan and are involved in all material decisions affecting the plan. The company sponsoring the plan is known as the "plan sponsor" and usually senior officers of the company serve as plan trustees or, the company hires an independent trustee. The plan document describes the design features and the operations of the plan. The Summary Plan Description, or SPD, describes in simple language the main provisions of the plan and must be distributed to plan participants. Every year the plan must file a tax return known as Form 5500 listing its assets, liabilities, and investment activity.

The Basic Structure of a 401(k)

401(k) and related sections refers to a specific section in the tax code that says employees can defer up to 100 percent of their salary to a maximum annual dollar amount of $11,000 and participants 50 years of age or older are also allowed to make special catch-up contributions.[3] Employee contributions are made on a pre-tax basis and grow tax-deferred until taken out. Businesses can deduct company contributions, including employee deferrals, employer matching, and employer discretionary contributions (e.g., profit sharing) and normal administrative expenses up to 25 percent of eligible payroll.[4]

We now turn our attention to a brief overview of the most common compliance tests surrounding 401(k) plans.

Annual 401(k) Tests

The Internal Revenue Code states that a qualified plan must not benefit Highly Compensated Employees (or HCEs, i.e., someone who earns more than $90,000 a year or is a 5 percent owner)[5] in a discriminatory manner. This includes "benefits," such as investment options, matching contributions, preferential access to accounts through loans or withdrawals, and the right to make certain levels of pre-tax deferrals. To ensure compliance, it requires the plan to be tested annually. Although the administrator running the plan usually performs these tests, a knowledge of how they are performed, the consequences of failing, and an explanation of how plan sponsors can correct a failed test, will help you design a plan that's right for your company.

AVERAGE DEFERRAL PERCENTAGE (ADP) TEST

The most basic test is the Average Deferral Percentage, or ADP test. Its purpose is to ensure that the HCEs do not save appreciably more as a percentage of pay than do the Non–Highly Compensated Employees (NHCEs). (In addition to the ADP test, a similar test is performed if an employer makes matching contributions. This test is known as the Average Contribution Percentage, or ACP test.)The test works like this:

+ **Step 1.** Calculate each eligible participant's average deferral percentage by dividing his deferrals by his salary.
+ **Step 2.** Separate all eligible employees into two groups: HCEs and NHCEs.
+ **Step 3.** Compare the average deferral percentages (ADP) of these groups. If the ADP of the HCEs does not exceed the ADP of the NHCEs by more than the allowable percentage, the test is satisfied. The basic test is 1.25 times the NHCE average but usually the HCEs can set aside up to 2 percent more as a class.[6]

Let's look at an example:

EMPLOYEE	COMPENSATION	EMPLOYEE CONTRIBUTION	DEFERRAL PERCENTAGE
A	$30,000	$0	0%
B	$20,000	$1,000	5% ($1,000/$20,000)
NHCE Totals	**$50,000**	**$1,000**	**2.5% average**
E	$90,000	$9,000	10% ($9,000/$90,000)
F	$100,000	$4,000	4% ($4,000/$100,000)
G	$110,000	$5,000	4.5% ($5,00/$110,000)
HCE Totals	**$300,000**	**$18,000**	**6.17% average**

In this example, if the HCEs as a group had averaged 4.5 percent or less (no more than 2 percent above the NHCEs rate), the test would have passed. But because the 6.17 percent rate far exceeds the NHCE rate of 2.5 percent, the test fails. To correct the failed test, the plan must either return excess contributions back to the HCEs, or make additional contributions for the benefit of NHCEs. Please note that eligible employees who choose not to participate have an ADP of 0 and, consequently, significantly lower the average savings percentage of their group. Lack of participation and low savings rates reduces the ADP of the NHCEs and potentially limits the amount the HCEs can contribute to the plan. This is an important lesson and one we will return to later in the book.

Solid plan design and effective communication will go a long way to ensure that your plan passes its annual tests. Employers can use the previous year's ADP/ACP data to guide HCEs in setting a savings level that is not excessive.[7]

Companies can also encourage greater savings by targeting newly eligible employees and nonparticipants to join the plan. The benefit is that fewer "zeroes" in the test and higher overall savings rates raise the ADP of the NHCEs, thus allowing the HCEs to save more. We will examine sound plan design principles in chapters 5 and 6 and discuss proven methods of increasing participation in chapter 10.

"Correcting" Failed ADP/ACP Tests

If a plan is determined to have failed either the ADP or ACP test, the plan is out of compliance and, unless corrected within a specific time period, could lose its tax-privileged status.[8] There are several ways to correct a failed ADP/ACP test.

The most common method to pass a failed ADP test is to simply refund the excess contributions to the HCEs. The returned money is considered taxable income to the employee. The return of excess savings doesn't cost the employer anything but it will limit the ability of the affected employees to save for retirement, and will increase their previous year's taxable income.

Other options are also available. Companies can rectify a failed ADP test by making a special one-time contribution, called a Qualified Non-Elective Contribution, or QNEC. In this option, employers make an end-of-the-year, 100 percent vested contribution to some or all NHCEs. For example, by making a contribution to the least highly paid NHCEs in an amount sufficient to pass the ADP test, the employer will raise the ADP of the NHCEs, allowing the HCEs to save their original percentage. Employers can also make Qualified Matching Contributions (QMAC); fully vested contributions that may be added to the employee's deferral to pass the ADP test.[9]

BUYING YOUR WAY OUT THROUGH PLAN DESIGN: SIMPLE, SAFE HARBOR AND "AUTOMATIC" ENROLLMENT

In chapter 2, "The Retirement Plan Universe," we saw that there are two types of 401(k) plans, SIMPLE and Safe Harbor, where the plan sponsor is able to circumvent annual ADP/ACP tests. This freedom, however, comes at a price. Both plans require a fixed, immediately vested annual employer contribution. In addition, the SIMPLE Plan limits participant contributions to $7,000 per year and is only available to companies with fewer than a hundred eligible employees.[10] For some companies, the Safe Harbor plan may simply cost too much, since it requires a 4-percent "effective" matching rate or 3-percent contribution to all eligibles.[11] For others, these new plans may signal welcome relief. If you are starting a plan, you should consider these alternatives. If you already have a plan in place but it has a history of chronic ADP/ACP problems, you may want to consider amending it to include a Safe Harbor design.[12]

"Negative" or "Automatic" Enrollment

"Negative" or "automatic" enrollment allows an employer to automatically enroll all eligible employees without first requiring them to fill out a salary reduction form.[13] After notifying all employees, the employer invests a specified percentage (usually in the 2 to 4 percent range)[14] of the participant's money in a "default" account, such as a balanced fund or short-term bond fund, or money market/stable value fund, until the participant decides how to invest his money. An employee can opt out by calling a 1-800 number or notifying his employer.

Although you must still conduct annual discrimination testing, automatic enrollment is effective at increasing participation and raising the overall savings rate of the NHCEs—the linchpin of passing 401(k) discrimination tests.[15] Used in the fast-food and hospitality industry for years, "automatic" enrollment was recently approved by the IRS so that the sponsor no longer has to file for an individual determination letter.[16] There are, however, several questions you might want to ask yourself before implementing automic enrollment.

+ **Define Goals**—What are your goals? If all you want to do is pass discrimination testing, there may be easier, more cost-effective ways to accomplish this, such as targeting nonparticipants, raising the match percentage, or making QNEC and QMAC contributions. If you are truly concerned about low participation and low savings of your workforce, especially among the lower-paid workers, then negative enrollment may be right for you.

+ **Current Plan Design**—If you currently provide an immediate vested, 3-percent matching contribution, it is easy to argue that employees who don't participate in the 401(k) are not only failing to prepare for retirement, but are missing an important benefit. If you don't match at all or the match is barebones, then it may be far more difficult to argue the case for negative enrollment, especially when the low-paid group doesn't have much tax incentive to defer.

+ **Average Deferral Percentage and Investments**[17]—The two big operational issues are (1) how much of the employee's salary do you set aside and (2) how do you invest their money? The most common "default" average deferral percentage is 3 percent found in 60 percent of plans. The most common "default" investment option is stable value, found in 46 percent of plans, with money market and balanced options tied for second and third at 20.8 percent each. (A word of caution here. Prudent investment management suggests picking either a balanced fund or an actively managed fund that invests in a mix of cash, bonds, and stock. Investing in a GIC or money market option may create an "opportunity loss.")

+ **404(c) Compliance**—ERISA Section 404(c) provides limited fiduciary relief to plan sponsors, assuming participants can exercise sufficient control over their accounts. It is designed specifically for participant-directed plans. In the case of negative enrollment, the plan sponsor makes investment decisions for those participants who do not exercise control over at least their initial investment selection (the "default" option). As a result, the plan is not 404(c)-compliant with respect to these employees.

✦ **Employee Education**—Negative enrollment doesn't replace education. If anything, it places greater demands on communicating the basics to all employees. It is important not to forget about the employees once they're in the plan.

Negative enrollment is a major plan-design commitment and is not for everyone. However, in the right situation it can make a dramatic difference in a plan's participation and savings rate—two essential pieces of a successful plan.

THE COST IMPLICATIONS OF REDRESSING TESTING PROBLEMS

The different methods of dealing with chronic testing problems have different cost implications. Below, I've listed the methods in the order of the least costly to the most expensive, generally speaking.

✦ Refund excess contributions to HCEs
✦ Targeted employee-education campaign
✦ QNEC & QMAC contributions
✦ Automatic ("negative") enrollment
✦ Safe Harbor/SIMPLE plan design

For many plan sponsors, Safe Harbor contributions represent a powerful tool to combat chronic ADP/ACP testing problems. Although they guarantee passage, they are also the most expensive. The trick is to weigh the costs and to compare them against the benefits gained. Companies have other means to fight testing problems, including careful plan design (e.g., eligibility, compensation, and matching contributions) as well as strong employee communication and education programs. Finally, "automatic" enrollment is another option to increase participation.

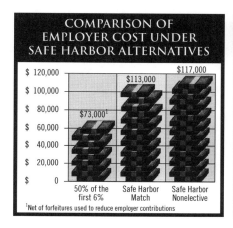

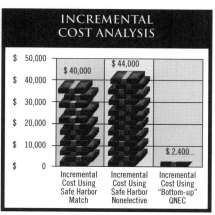

EXAMPLE: XYZ Company sponsors a 401(k) plan that includes 88 eligible employees, and has failed both the ADP and actual contribution percentage (ACP) tests in the past. The plan is again projected to fail, with distributions required to each of the eight HCEs. The matching contribution under the current formula is projected to be approximately $78,000.

If the plan were to implement the safe harbor matching formula of 100% of the first 3% of compensation, and 50% of the next 2% of compensation, the allocation is projected to increase by $35,000 to $113,000.

The plan above currently applies a seven-year graded vesting. Each year, there are approximately $5,000 in forfeitures of nonvested matching contributions that XYZ Company uses to reduce the required employer contributions. Since the safe harbor requires 100% vesting, costs are increased by the previously forfeited amounts. Alternately, the plan could use the nonelective safe harbor contribution. In the above example, the cost of this type of contribution would be $117,000. This contribution must be allocated to each eligible employee, regardless of whether or not that employee actually participated in the plan.[18]

OTHER ANNUAL TESTS

The ADP and ACP tests are, without a doubt, the most important 401(k) compliance tests. Although passage of these tests is essential to a well-run plan, there are other tests to be familiar with. Neglecting these other tests could be detrimental to the success of your plan.

❖   ❖   ❖

Minimum Coverage (IRS Section 410b)

The Coverage Test is designed to ensure that the plan is offered to different groups of employees and not just the owners or the HCEs. With respect to 401(k) plans, benefitting and participating are not the same thing. An eligible employee who elects not to participate, is still "benefitting" (i.e., the plan is being offered to her) even though she chooses not to participate in the plan. The key measurement in the Coverage Test is the ratio percentage, which compares the coverage percentages of the HCEs and NHCEs. Generally, if a plan does not exclude any employee groups who meet its age and service requirements, other than non–resident aliens or union groups, this test is passed.[19]

401(k) Elective Deferrals

The maximum annual 401(k) dollar contribution per participant is $11,000 in 2002. This number goes up in $1,000 increments until it reaches $15,000 in 2006 and is then indexed for inflation. It is important to monitor this limit and to stop employee contributions once it has been passed.

Annual Addition Test (IRC Section 415 limits)

The Internal Revenue Code (IRC) limits the amount a participant can set aside each tax year to $11,000. The combined maximum employee and employer contributions including forfeitures that can go into a participant's account cannot exceed the lesser of $40,000 or 100 percent of pay. Contributions include all of the following:

+ Pre-tax employee salary deferrals
+ Employer-matching contributions
+ Discretionary profit-sharing contributions

✦ Post-tax employee contributions
✦ Plan forfeitures (if allocated back to participants)

MAXIMUM COMPENSATION LIMIT (IRC SECTION 401(A)(17))

A plan can only consider the first $200,000 of an employee's compensation for matching and deferral purposes. Any amount over $200,000 is excluded from consideration.

TOP-HEAVY TEST (IRC SECTION 416)

A plan also needs to be tested to make sure it is not "top-heavy," i.e., "key" employees control in excess of 60 percent of the vested plan assets. The smaller the company and the larger the number of owners, the more likely it is that a plan may be top-heavy. (As mentioned before, "key" and "HCE" employees have different definitions and can refer to separate people within a plan.) A key employee is someone who falls into one of the categories listed below:

✦ Employees who own more than 5 percent of the company
✦ Employees who own more than 1 percent of the company and earn more than $150,000 in compensation
✦ Any officer with compensation greater than $130,000

Top-heavy problems are commonly found in professional associations like law firms and doctors' offices, where the income gap between the professionals and the staff is wide. If a plan is determined to be top-heavy, certain minimum contributions—usually equal to 3 percent of compensation—must be made to non–key employees, and employer contributions must vest at a rate at least as fast as a six-year graded schedule or a three-year cliff schedule.

SPONSOR DEDUCTIBLE CONTRIBUTION LIMIT

The maximum tax-deductible employer limit is 25 percent of eligible compensation. This includes all employee (pre- and post-tax) and employer (matching, profit sharing, and forfeiture) contributions. Passing this test is usually only a concern when the sponsor offers a combination profit-sharing/401(k) plan, and the profit-sharing contribution percentage is quite generous, say, more than 15 percent.

This chapter has examined the annual compliance tests common to 401(k) plans. The framework for 401(k) is solidly built. It's a structure intended to safeguard the money, hopes and dreams of the millions of people who are investing for their retirement. Now, with the basic structure in place, we're ready to consider the subject of customization—designing a plan that fits the needs of your particular company.

Notes

1. Treas. Reg. §§ 1.401-1(a)(2); 1.401-1(a)(3); 1.401-1(a)(3)(ii); 1.401-1(a)(3)(v); 1.401-1(b)(2).

2. Segregating plan assets from company assets is important as plan assets are not subject to creditor's claims in the event of corporate bankruptcy.

3. For 401(k), 403(b) and 457(b) plans, the maximum contribution is $11,000 in 2002, $12,000 in 2003, $13,000 in 2004, $14,000 in 2005, and $15,000 in 2006. Individuals aged 50 or older will also be allowed to make additional "catch up" contributions of $1,000 in 2002, $2,000 in 2003, $3,000 in 2004, $4,000 in 2005, and $5,000 in 2006. Diversified Investment Advisors, "Economic Growth and Tax Relief Reconciliation Act of 2001 (EGTRRA)," p. 2. 401(k)—elective deferrals; 415(c)(1)— 100% of salary; 402(g)(1)—$11,000 limit; EGTRRA—$1,000 catch-up.

4. Includable compensation is defined by each plan in its plan document, but for most plans it means W-2 income up to $200,000. See IRC §414(q)(1).

5. *www.psca.org/glossary.html*. See IRC §414(q)(1).

6. (1) less than 2 percent (no more than 2 times the NHCE contribution percent); (2) greater than 8 percent (if NHCE average percentage contribution is greater than 8 percent, the HCE average percentage is limited to 1.25 times the NHCE average). See IRC §401(m)(2)(A).

7. ADP and ACP tests are performed based on the elective deferrals and contributions for the Non–Highly Compensated Employees for the plan year preceding the plan year being tested, rather than those made for the testing year. An employer may elect to use data for the testing year, rather than the preceding plan year, but if the employer makes this election, it may only be changed as provided by the IRS.

   For a plan's first year, the ADP of Non–Highly Compensated Employees shall be deemed to be 3 percent for the preceding plan year, unless the employer elects to use the actual ADP for the first plan year. A similar rule applies for the ACP test. (Briggs & Morgan—http://www.briggs.com/alerthp.htm February 16, 2001.)

8. A 1995 Hewitt Associates Survey "found that 61% of 401(k) plans discovered that the contributions of highly compensated employees must be restricted or adjusted as a result of nondiscrimination testing." *http://401k-administration.com/administration.html,* "Administration of 401(k) Plans," February 20, 2002.

9. ". . . an employee earning $20,000 annually who makes a $350 contribution to receive the core $350 QMAC is treated as having a salary deferral of 3.5% ($700/$20,000)." "Revisiting 401(k) Design Issues," *401(k) Advisor,* v. 7, no. 8, August 2000.

10. $7,000 in 2002, $8,000 in 2003, $9,000 in 2004, $10,000 in 2005, and then subject to cost-of-living adjustments in $500 increments. Individuals aged 50 or older will also be allowed to make additional "catch up" contributions of $1,000 in 2002, $2,000 in 2003, $3,000 in 2004, $4,000 in 2005, and $5,000 in 2006. Diversified Investment Advisors, "Economic Growth and Tax Relief Reconciliation Act of 2001 (EGTRRA)," p. 2.

11. The plan can make an immediately vested 3-percent contribution to all NHCEs who are eligible to participate in the 401(k) plan. Alternatively, the employer may elect to make immediately vested matching contributions to NHCEs equal to 100 percent

of the first 3 percent of employee contributions, plus 50 percent of the next 2 percent of employee contributions. See §401(k)(12).

12. See note 23, page 37–38.

13. "The IRS has issued a regulatory bulletin (Internal Revenue Bulletin No. 2000-7, February 14, 2000) on automatic enrollment requiring the following:

+ Advance notice to the employee of the automatic enrollment feature and the ability of the employee to "opt out"
+ Reasonable time for the employee to "opt out" after receiving the notice
+ Ability for the participant to stop or change contributions in the future
+ Annual notification to the participant of the average deferral percentage and the right to change it"

"*Automatic Enrollment: Benefits and Costs of Adoption*", The Vanguard Center for Retirement Research, May 2001, p.2.

14. The most common default deferral rate is 3 percent found in 60 percent of the surveyed plans. "Automatic Enrollment, 2001," Profit Sharing/401(k) Council of America.

15. "Among companies that provided both a current plan participation rate and a plan participation rate from one year ago, participation rose from an average of 75.7% to 81.3%." "Automatic Enrollment, 2001," Profit Sharing/401(k) Council of America.

16. IRS revenue ruling (98-30), *CFO Magazine,* September 1998, p. 30.

17. "Automatic Enrollment 2001 Study," Profit Sharing/401(k) Council of America.

18. "The Safe Harbor Contribution Formulas—Are the Benefits Worth the Cost?," *Connections*, Fidelity Investments, Spring 1998.

19. "Section 410(b) of the Tax Code allows a retirement plan to be qualified as long as the percentage of non-highly compensated employees covered under the plan is at

least 70% of the percentage of highly compensated employees covered under the plan. For example, if 100% of a company's HCEs are covered, which is typical, then 70% of the NHCEs must be covered. Employees can be carved out as long as the plan document spells out clearly which groups of employees or which company divisions is being excluded. Specifically named employees cannot be carved out. Instead, for example, all clerical employees and grounds keepers can be excluded." *401(k) Today: Designing, Maintaining & Maximizing Your Company's Plan*, Stephen J. Butler, Berrett-Koehler Publishers, San Francisco, 1999, p. 115.

CHAPTER 5

401(k) Plan Design, Part I

No two companies are the same, and no two companies' retirement plan objectives are exactly the same either. Good plan design should reflect the realities of your company and strike a balance between customization and administrative simplicity. Achieving this balance is well worth the effort. The major elements of plan design include eligibility, compensation, vesting, and employer contributions. These are the key variables that shape the plan and contribute to its success or failure. By doing a little more work on the front end, common problems can be avoided.

A successful 401(k) plan has, as its foundation, a well thought-out design that makes sense for both the participants who use it and the people who administer it. "Simple but not too simple" is a proven design principle. Good design is also dynamic. As companies and 401(k) regulations change over time, plan design should be reviewed and updated as necessary. This chapter will look at the many ways plans can be assembled and the provisions within a plan that can be customized. The purpose is to give you an overview of how these parts can work together to accomplish your objectives.

✦ ✦ ✦

PLAN DOCUMENTS

ERISA requires that all plans must be in writing, i.e., that a plan document be maintained. These documents can differ in the degree of flexibility they offer the sponsoring employer. The main types of plan documents are Prototype, Volume Submitter, and Custom. The choice of the plan document depends on the sponsor's needs for investment and design flexibility as well as the cost of document preparation and IRS submission, and the costs of ongoing compliance with legislative and regulatory changes.

PROTOTYPE PLAN DOCUMENTS

These are the most common plan documents, and they offer several advantages. First, they have already been reviewed and preapproved by the IRS. As legislation changes, it is incumbent on the service providers who offer them—like banks, insurance companies, and mutual fund firms—to incorporate these changes into the plan and to receive approval from the IRS, thereby eliminating the need of the plan sponsor to do so. As a result, prototypes are less expensive than any other document and are the document of choice for most plan sponsors.

A prototype usually has two parts: the adoption agreement and the plan-and-trust document. The plan-and-trust document contains all the nonelective provisions applicable to all adopting employers, while the trust provisions of the document details the responsibilities of the trustee who maintains the assets.

The adoption agreement controls the main plan design elements, and the employer can customize the plan by selecting among a well-defined set of options. For example, sponsors control such features as eligibility, employer match amount and frequency, vesting, loans, and the investments to be offered. Once approved, however, an employer can only amend the plan by selecting options already permitted in the adoption agreement. Any other amendment will generally require a customized document and approval from the IRS.

STANDARD AND NONSTANDARD PROTOTYPE PLANS

There are two kinds of prototype adoption agreements: "standardized" and "nonstandardized." The nonstandardized variety allows for greater flexibility than the standardized version.[1] For example, a company would use a nonstandardized document if they wished to incorporate one of the following design features:

+ Exclude certain forms of compensation, such as overtime, bonuses, and commissions, from the plan document's definition of compensation.
+ Exclude certain classes of employees, such as union members and nonresident aliens.
+ Require employees to be employed on the last day of the plan year and/or work at least 1,000 hours in order to receive employer contributions.

Standard and nonstandard prototype plan documents are the most popular because they shift responsibility of keeping the plan document compliant and up-to-date to the service provider.[2] If you need greater flexibility, however, there are other options.

VOLUME SUBMITTER

Volume Submitter plans lie somewhere between the boilerplate language of a prototype document and the tailoring of a custom document. Like a prototype plan, it allows some modification. And like a prototype document, it is also less expensive to file and maintain than a custom document. Although it can be structured like a prototype with a basic plan document and an adoption agreement, it can also be written as a single document that reflects the plan design provisions of the adopting employer. The main advantage of a volume submitter plan over a prototype plan is that changes can be made to it without automatically turning it into an individually designed (i.e., "custom") plan.

CUSTOM PLAN DOCUMENTS

These documents allow for the most flexibility since they are written for a specific plan. Usually drafted by lawyers, they allow the sponsor to customize virtually every aspect of the plan. However, they are more expensive to execute and may require approval from the IRS. Also, as IRS rules governing retirement plans change over time, these plans must be updated on an individual basis and at the plan sponsor's expense. Unless you require significant rewording of standard provisions found in prototype and volume submitter documents, custom plan documents are best left alone.

BASIC PLAN PROVISIONS

Regardless of the plan document you select, you will need to address certain critical design components.

1. Effective Date

A plan can be effective on any date. It's not necessary to use the first day of the calendar year. The plan must, however, be in place before a company begins withholding any employee-deferral money.

2. Plan Year

The plan year can be any twelve-month period; for example, the company's fiscal year. The employer should select the plan year–end to coincide with obtaining data to complete Form 5500 and the discrimination testing (e.g., W-2 data, eligibility, etc.). For that reason, a calendar-year plan year is the most common. Many employers also elect to use a calendar year because of the timing of ADP/ACP test results. If refunds need to be made to HCEs, use of a noncalendar plan year can make it necessary for the refund recipients to refile their prior year's tax return.

3. Trustee

A trustee receives, holds, and distributes plan assets according to the plan provisions, and ensures the accurate transmission and allocation of investment contributions. All 401(k) plans, regardless of the service provider, must have a trustee. Depending on the plan, a trustee's role can range from having complete discretion over the selection of plan investments to being a mere custodian. A plan may name an individual as a trustee (a "named" trustee) or use a corporate trustee, such as a bank or trust company.[3] Today, most corporate trustees act only as custodians and are sometimes called "nondiscretionary" or "directed" trustees.[4] I usually recommend the use of corporate trustee services if they are built into the vendor's package and are reasonably priced.

4. Definition of Compensation

The law requires that a nondiscriminatory definition of compensation be used. The IRS has several safe harbor definitions that are acceptable, but the most widely used one, Section 3401(a), is based on W-2 compensation—a number that most employers track. In a nonstandardized adoption agreement, the plan sponsor can exclude compensation such as overtime, bonus, and commission. In most situations, I don't recommend excluding these forms of compensation, since it limits the participants' ability to save based on their total compensation.

5. Eligibility

All employees are eligible to join once they have met minimum age and service standards.[5] It used to be that most plans imposed the maximum statutory age and service restrictions for eligibility (e.g., age 21 and one year of service) in order to increase the likelihood of passing their ADP/ACP tests.[6] This is changing. Because of the ability to use the previous year's testing data ("look back" provision), the ability to exclude eligible employees under age 21 from annual testing[7] and the need to gain a competitive edge in recruiting, more and more plan sponsors are reducing their eligibility requirements to six months and three months of service.[8] In some industries, such as the tech sector, it's common to see immediate eligibility.

Eligibility also allows you to specify which groups of employees will be included in the plan. Certain groups, such as nonresident aliens, and employees covered under a collective bargaining agreement, can be excluded from eligibility. The reason for their exclusion is straightforward; nonresident aliens may not be long-term employees, and union employees are usually eligible for other union-sponsored retirement plans.

6. Entry Dates

If the waiting period for eligibility is one year, the plan must allow for at least two entry dates per plan year. If the waiting period is six months or less, it's OK to have only one entry date per year. Most plans offer either semi-annual or quarterly entry dates although with the increase in online enrollment, more frequent entry dates are becoming more common (e.g., immediate or monthly).

7. Maximum Deferral Percentage (MDP) and Maximum Contributions

A stand-alone 401(k) allows participants to set aside up to 100 percent of compensation to an annual dollar maximum of $11,000, or whichever is less. For plans that include other contribution sources besides 401(k) (e.g., matching, profit sharing, after-tax, etc.), the total dollar amount cannot exceed $40,000 as this is the overall limit for defined-contribution plans. If you already have a plan, you may wish to either eliminate the maximum deferral percentage or raise it substantially to allow for greater savings, especially among the low and moderate wage earners.

8. After-Tax Contributions

Some plans allow participants to set money aside "after-tax." In this situation, the employee's money goes into the plan after federal and state taxes have been paid. The money grows tax-deferred and is then taken out tax-free at retirement.[9]

The ability to defer on an after-tax basis is a wonderful feature for those who can afford it. For the participant who can maximize his pre-tax deferral and still set aside money on a post-tax basis, meeting one's retirement goals should be easy. Post-tax deferrals are included in the Annual Contribution Percentage (ACP) test along with employer-matching contributions. Since it is the HCEs who are most likely to take advantage of post-tax savings, it could complicate the ACP test. If you already have a plan, you can look at your previous year's ACP test result to make this determination. If you easily passed the test, you might want to consider adding post-tax deferrals. If you failed it, you may want to forget about it. Also, because of the explosion in recent years of different types of IRAs and specifically the Roth IRA, there may be better after-tax methods to save for retirement.

9. Rollover/Transfer Contributions

The law allows for both rollover and transfer contributions to be made to the plan.

Although people use the words interchangeably, they have separate technical definitions. Rollover contributions come from a "rollover" or "conduit" IRA (i.e., they hold qualified plan assets only) while transfers come from another plan and retain all of the rights and protected benefit provisions of that plan. Rollovers and transfers do not count toward the annual maximum deferral amount. Most plans allow for both rollovers and transfers, which enables employees to keep all of their retirement assets under one roof. And with the passage of EGTRRA, even employees who have money in 403(b) and 457 plans may now be able to roll it over to their new employer's 401(k)!

10. Retirement Age

The definition of Normal or Early Retirement Age (ERA) is not a critical design issue. It is common to have the Normal Retirement Age set at age 65. By law, employees are allowed to take distributions from their 401(k) accounts at age 59½ without paying penalties. An Early Retirement Age provision is good if the company wants to encourage older employees to leave the company. An ERA provision, for example, age 55, allows the participant to take money from the plan sooner than age 59½ without paying penalties.

11. Forfeitures

Forfeitures refer to the unvested employer contributions "forfeited" back to the plan after a participant leaves. Forfeited monies are lumped into a single account and tracked as a separate money type by the recordkeeper. They can be used to reduce future employer contributions, a common practice, or they can be reallocated among remaining participants. They can also be used to reduce plan expenses.

12. Loans

Participant loans are a popular feature.[10] A loan allows participants to borrow as much as 50 percent of their vested account balance up to $50,000 without having to pay any taxes or penalties. For example, a vested account balance of $20,000 means that the participant may borrow up to $10,000.

The specific rules governing loans are spelled out in the loan policy statement. For example, many plans usually require a minimum loan amount, e.g., $1,000, in order to prevent "frivolous" loans. The loan must bear a "reasonable rate of interest," which most loan agreements define as the prime rate plus 1 to 2 percent. The maximum loan period is five years, except when the loan money is used for the purchase of a primary residence, in which case the IRS says the loan must be repaid within a "reasonable" period of time.[11] After the loan is processed, an amortization table is created based on the repayment period and the interest rate. The participant repays the money through payroll deductions based on the loan schedule.

I highly recommend a loan provision, since it allows employees access to their money and is a way to encourage younger employees to join the plan. Plans that allow loans have higher participation and savings rates than those that don't. However, despite the apparent advantages of borrowing from yourself and becoming your own lender, loans are an expensive source of money and should not be encouraged.[12] Sponsors can take several steps to restrict loan usage such as allowing only one loan at a time, allowing only one loan per year and requiring the employee to pay the cost of the loan-processing fee.

13. Hardship Withdrawals

401(k) plans allow for the early distribution of retirement money due to extreme financial hardship. The hardship withdrawal is subject to a 20-percent income tax withholding and a 10 percent penalty.[13] Hardship withdrawals are granted using one of the two sets of criteria:

Safe Harbor Method
+ Costs related to the purchase of a participant's principal residence
+ Payment to prevent eviction from or foreclosure on the participant's principal residence
+ Payment of medical expenses incurred by the participant or the participant's spouse or dependents
+ Payment of tuition for post-secondary education by the participant or the participant's spouse or dependents

Facts and Circumstances Method

Under this method, the reasons are expanded to include other heavy and immediate needs of the employee. The Facts and Circumstances method requires the participant to submit written evidence to the plan in order to prove the need and document the inability to meet the need through other sources. This method involves more of the employer's time and effort to ensure compliance with the law.[14]

I recommend use of the Safe Harbor method in cases of hardship withdrawal whenever possible, because it is relatively easy to administer. Also, in a situation where a participant does not meet the Safe Harbor definition, the plan sponsor can shift the onus of denial to the IRS.

14. In-Service Withdrawals

This provision provides a loophole for those who want to take some money out of their plan while still working or "in service" but do not qualify under the hardship provisions. Here's how it works. A participant withdraws money from her 401(k) and rolls the money to an IRA.[16] Once the money goes into the IRA, she can take the money out as long as she pays the taxes and the 10-percent penalty, assuming she's younger than 59½. In general, an In-Service Withdrawal adds distribution flexibility to the plan and allows participants (especially younger ones) another way to access their money.

Now we turn our attention to one of the biggest plan design issues of all: employer contributions.

Notes

1. Besides plan design flexibility, there is another difference. Standardized adoption agreements are designed to satisfy coverage and nondiscrimination requirements of the IRC and do not require the user to file for an IRS determination letter if the employer has never maintained another type of qualified plan (e.g., profit sharing, money purchase, etc.) Nonstandardized agreements do require the filing of a determination letter.

2. An added benefit of standardized and nonstandardized prototypes and volume sub-mitter documents is that you may rely on the plan document sponsor's IRS letter of determination, assuming you do not add any non-IRS-approved language to the document.

3. Overall, 43.7 percent of plans are self-trusteed, and 30 percent use banks.

4. Plan sponsors who use a third-party corporate trustee to try to transfer their fiduci-ary liability are generally not successful. Whenever there is a problem involving the performance of trustee duties, the corporate trustees can argue that they only per-form a ministerial task for the plan and are only acting on directions received either from the employer or the plan participants. This argument is usually successful.

5. The IRS defines a year of service (both for vesting and for eligibility purposes) to be one in which the employee is credited with 1,000 or more hours of work in a twelve-month consecutive period. IRC §410(a)(3)(A). Some employers have a hard time tracking actual hours. The IRS allows for a method of tracking hours based on "equiv-alency." Use of the equivalency method will result in a more generous calculation than if actual hours were counted. Treas. Reg. §1.410(a)-7; DOL Reg. §2530.200b-3.

   The following conversion factors are used in the equivalency method:

   ✦ Days worked: For any day an employee works at least one hour, the employee will be credited with 10 hours.
   ✦ Weeks worked: For any week an employee works at least one hour, the employee will be credited with 45 hours.
   ✦ Semi-monthly payroll periods: For any semi-monthly period an employee works at least one hour, the employee will be credited with 95 hours.
   ✦ Months worked: For any month an employee works at least one hour, the employee will be credited with 190 hours.

   The equivalency method is only recommended for employers who find it diffi-cult or impossible to track actual hours.

6. Employees cannot be excluded if they have attained age 21, and employees cannot be required to wait more than one year to become eligible. See IRC §410(a)(3)(A).

7. As of January 1, 1998, employees under the age of 21 and less than one year of service can now be considered eligible to participate in the plan without being considered eligible for purposes of the ADP/ACP tests. This should help companies with younger, low-wage workforces. It should be pointed out, however, that it becomes an administrative burden to enroll employees only to have them quickly terminate.

8. According to William M. Mercer's 2000–2001 Survey on Employee Savings Plan:

   ✦ Almost 70 percent of the sample have eligibility requirements of three months of a service or less.
   ✦ 37 percent offer eligibility after hire, provided age requirements have been met.
   ✦ 43 percent of all plans have no age requirement.
   ✦ 19 percent of plans have immediate eligibility, with no age or service requirements.

   http://www.plansponsor.com/eprise/main/Plansponsor/News/HR/MercerVestingMatch, December 27, 2001.
       "Immediate" eligibility increased from 24 percent in 1998 to 37 percent in 2001, and eligibility of three months or less increased from 32 percent in 1998 to 55 percent in 2001. Profit-sharing plan Eligibility Survey 2001 by the Profit Sharing/401(k) Council of America.

9. "A worker under age 59½ may withdraw after-tax contributions from his 401(k) plan without paying a penalty or obvious taxes. . . . But when it comes to the earnings on after-tax, he must still pay taxes and a 10% penalty." "Why a 401(k) Option May Deserve a Look," *New York Times,* November 24, 1996.

10. Most service providers' plan documents define "reasonable" as ten, fifteen, or twenty years.

11. Although loans are widespread, participants should be cautioned against using them. First, they are taking money out of the marketplace, which in a rising market means that they will likely experience an "opportunity" cost. Second, the money

they use to pay back the loan is after-tax money. When they draw down their 401(k) savings during retirement, the money they used to pay back the loan will be taxed twice. If at all possible, participants should try to access lower-cost money first, such as home equity loans and margin loans before taking out a loan. Also, if a participant quits or is let go, the amount of the outstanding loan balance must be paid back, usually immediately. If the participant can't pay it back, it is considered a premature distribution and is subject to taxes and penalties.

12. "The amount distributed under the hardship rules must not exceed the amount of need. See Treas. Reg. §1.401(k)-d(1)(iii)(B). The distribution may be 'grossed up' by an amount necessary to pay federal, state, or local income taxes and any penalties resulting from the distribution. Although the law no longer requires the 20% mandatory withholding on 401(k) hardship withdrawals of elective contributions, all applicable taxes due on the amount may be considered when determining the amount of need. Most hardship distributions are subject to a 10% early withdrawal penalty tax, but limited exceptions exist." "Hardship Withdrawals, Step by Step," Richard J. Levesque, *Defined Contribution Focus*, Spring 2000.

13. The regulations provide two methods for determining whether each of these conditions is met. For example, a plan sponsor that wants flexibility in stating the available guidelines for hardships but also wants to avoid a personal review of an employee's finances should adopt the Facts and Circumstances determination for the "immediate and heavy" condition, and the Safe Harbor determination for the "amount necessary" condition.

"The Facts and Circumstances determination is based on all relevant facts and circumstances being considered in determining whether the "immediate and heavy" or the "amount necessary" conditions are satisfied. With regard to determining whether an immediate and heavy need exists, a plan should establish written guidelines for what constitutes an acceptable hardship. The criteria should be precise and should not discriminate in favor of highly compensated employees. The regulations specifically note that the need to purchase material objects such as a boat or car would not meet this standard, but funeral expenses would." "Hardship Withdrawals, Step by Step," Richard J. Levesque, *Defined Contribution Focus*, Spring 2000. See Treas. Reg. §1.401(k)-(d)(1)(iii).

Q 3:81 What are the facts and circumstances rules for hardship withdrawals?

A: *The employer must determine whether an immediate and heavy financial need exists based on all relevant facts and circumstances. Under this general rule, the employer can decide on the amount necessary to satisfy the financial need either by using a general Facts and Circumstances test, or by using a reasonable reliance test where the employer relies on the participant's written representation that the need cannot be satisfied from other sources. See Treas. Reg. §1.401(k)-(d)(1)(iii).*

—*401(k) Answer Book*, 1997 Edition

14. The money can be moved in one of two ways. "You can do a trustee-to-trustee transfer in which the employer moves the money directly to the IRA. . . . The other option is to take the distribution with the 20% withholding, make up the 20% and deposit the full amount into the IRA. An employee who takes that route will recover the 20% when he files his taxes." "Trap Doors and Back Doors," Mary Rowland, *Dow Jones Investment Advisor,* February 1998.

CHAPTER 6

PLAN DESIGN, PART II:

EMPLOYER-MATCHING CONTRIBUTIONS

Deciding on whether or not to contribute to the plan, how much to contribute, and how to structure the contribution(s), are some of the biggest design decisions an employer makes. Employer contributions have a direct bearing on participation and savings percentage—two essential criteria of a "successful" plan.

As we discussed before, 401(k) contributions are fundamentally employee money. Employers are not required to contribute to a 401(k) plan although most do. It is the low-cost and flexible nature of these plans that explains much of their appeal. Some companies that cannot commit to making contributions at the inception of the plan start the plan with the idea of contributing later. Companies that have hybrid 401(k)/profit-sharing plan designs may make a modest profit-sharing contribution (e.g., 1 to 4 percent) to all employees but make no 401(k) matching contribution. (If you recall from chapter 2, profit-sharing contributions go to all eligible employees regardless of whether they participate in the 401(k) plan, whereas matching contributions only go to employees who contribute to the 401(k) plan.) Other companies make a regular 401(k) matching contribution and only contribute to the profit-sharing plan when the company has an exceptionally strong fiscal year.

To Contribute or Not to Contribute?

Even though plan sponsors are not required to contribute, most do. Eighty percent of employers match with the most common formula of $0.50 of each dollar up to 6 percent of pay.[1] That's an "effective" matching rate of 3 percent ($.50 × 6% = 3%.)

There are several advantages to matching:

+ A matching contribution is the single most effective tool for increasing participation and raising a plan's overall savings rate and, therefore, your employee's financial security.
+ An increase in participation and savings percentage can help a plan pass its annual discrimination testing.
+ An employer match raises the general awareness of the plan especially when it is well communicated to employees.
+ Matching doesn't have to cost a fortune to be effective.

Let's examine each of these points in more detail.

Matching Works

A few years ago, a national benefits consulting firm performed a study that looked at participation rates at various levels of employer matching.[2] As you can see from the graph below, plans that match have higher participation rates across all income levels. The data also shows that a "reasonable" match coupled with strong communication program can lead to the same level of participation as a "rich" match with little or no communication. A matching contribution will have its greatest impact on participation at the lower and middle levels of the salary ranges. These are precisely the kinds of people for whom the plan was intended and who you want to join the plan in order to pass annual discrimination testing.

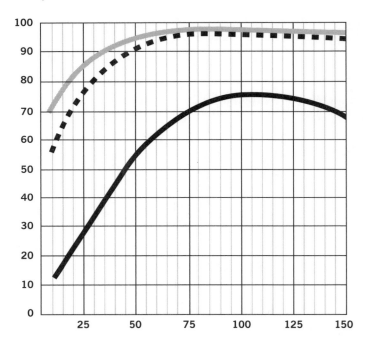

401(k) PARTICIPATION Rates by Wage under Alternate Communications and Matching Programs[3]

Participation Rate (% of Workforce)

Wage (in thousands of dollars)

━━━━━ 100% Match, No Communications

■ ■ ■ 25% Match, Targeted Communications

━━━━━ 25% Match, No Communications

Types of Matching Contributions: Fixed and Discretionary, Percent of Pay, Graded, Flat Dollar Amount

Employer contributions come in many different shapes and sizes, and a smart plan sponsor will tailor the contribution strategy to advance the overall goals of the retirement plan. There are several general comments to make about employer contributions:

+ Only "hybrid" plans allow for both profit sharing and 401(k) matching contributions.
+ Profit-sharing contributions go to all eligible employees, whereas 401(k) matching contributions go only to those employees who participate in the plan.
+ A plan sponsor can combine various contributions to create a customized strategy designed to advance the goals of the retirement program.

For example, the plan sponsor could make a fixed 3-percent profit-sharing contribution to create a baseline contribution for all eligible employees. He could then make an additional profit-sharing contribution of 3 percent if certain corporate goals are met, such as gross sales or return on equity. Finally, to reward employees who save on their own, he could match $.50 of each dollar put into the 401(k) plan. Below is an overview of different types of 401(k) employer-matching contributions.

+ Fixed—The plan sponsor establishes a contribution formula and writes it into the plan document. Only when the plan is formally amended can this formula be changed. A fixed match puts the plan sponsor on the hook for making the contribution.

+ Discretionary—The sponsor decides annually whether to contribute and how much to contribute. As a cost-saving measure, he can insist that only people who are employed on the last day of the plan year will receive the contribution ("Last Day Rule").

A discretionary match is well suited for companies with fluctuating cash flows that want to tie contributions to some larger corporate goal.

✦ **Percent of Pay**—The sponsor creates a formula based on a percentage of each employee's pay; for example, $.50 of each dollar to a maximum of 6 percent of pay. This contribution method is popular because it is easy to calculate and easy to administer.

✦ **Graded**—The sponsor contributes on the basis of a percentage of pay but weights the contribution either up or down. For example, $1 for each of the employee's first 3 percent; then $.50 on the next 3 percent. A graded match is well suited for a company that wants to reward the low savers.

✦ **Flat Dollar Amount**—The sponsor gives everyone a flat dollar amount or caps the percent of pay contribution with a flat dollar amount (e.g., dollar for dollar to 4 percent capped at $1,500). This allows the plan sponsor to easily limit the cost of the match.

COMPANY STOCK

Although most companies use cash when making matching contributions, for many large public companies contributions in the form of company stock are common.[4] The Enron 401(k) scandal, however, exposes the inherent fiduciary dangers of matching in company stock.

Corporations have a financial and managerial incentive to offer shares of stock over cash as the basis of the employer match. Because companies receive the same tax deduction for putting a $20 share of stock into a 401(k) as they do for putting $20 of cash into the plan, it is the cheapest form of employer-matching contribution short of not making one at all. Using company stock allows the company to conserve cash, a precious corporate resource. Also, large numbers of shares end up in employees' hands over time—investors who aren't likely to sell when the company announces bad news, especially if the company imposes restrictions on selling. Finally, employee ownership of large chunks of company stock helps reduce the risk of hostile takeovers and "unfriendly" shareholder resolutions.

The problem occurs when employees receive their match in company stock, are restricted from selling shares, and are also allowed to buy additional shares of stock as a stand-alone investment option within the plan. Unfortunately, many participants' account balances become over-concentrated in a single security; a recipe for financial disaster should the stock fall in value.

If you do decide to make matching contributions using company stock, allow participants to sell the stock within a reasonable period of time. If the match is also coupled with the security as a stand-alone investment option, inform participants about the inherent risk associated with overconcentration in a single security. This is your fiduciary obligation.

TOP-HEAVY PLANS

For smaller companies and many professionals, the overriding concern of plan design is often maximizing the owner's contributions. There are effective ways to maximize the owner's contributions including "integrated," "age-weighted," and "permitted disparity" profit-sharing plans. (We discussed these plans in more detail in chapter 2.) Plans of this nature give more of the profit-sharing contribution to older, more highly paid employees. Since small professional service organizations are far more likely to be "top-heavy" (i.e., 60 percent or more of the plan's assets are held by "key" employees) than larger firms, their contribution strategy is often determined by their "top-heavy" status. Top-heavy plans must make a 3-percent contribution of pay to all eligible employees.

For larger companies where the individual owner is not the overriding concern, other factors, such as competitive benchmarks, the nature of the job market, and a company's entire benefits package, help to shape its contribution strategy.

HOW MUCH TO CONTRIBUTE?

Once you decide on the contribution and its nature, the next question to consider is how much should the company contribute. For the most part, the answer is straightforward: How much can the company afford? But another part of the answer is more complex and is related to the company's retirement plan goals and the company's total compensation package. Do you want to reward employees for saving or are you more interested in creating a well-defined retirement benefit? How do contributions to a retirement plan fit into your overall compensation structure?

Again, the study (on page 84) on employer matching is helpful since it illustrates the diminishing returns that raising a match has on the participation rate. In other words, as you increase the match in absolute terms, the number of people who either begin to participate or raise their savings percentage begins to level off. This suggests that there is an optimal point for each plan where a plan sponsor can capture the majority of the match's effect. It should come as no surprise then that this point is largely determined by each company's demographics, such as average salaries and ages. In general, the more money people earn, the more money they have to save. For example, in a low-wage industry, a dollar-to-dollar match on the first 4 percent of pay may have a powerful effect on increasing participation. In a high-salary industry, however, a lower matching formula (e.g., $.50 to 6 percent) may have the same effect.

ESTIMATING THE COST OF A MATCH—IT'S NOT AS HARD OR AS MUCH AS YOU THINK

Estimating the cost of a match is easy. If you are going to use a percentage of pay, the first step is to convert the match formula into a baseline match percentage. For example, if the formula is $.50 match up to 6 percent of pay, that's the same as 3 percent of pay (.50 × 6% = 3%). If there are forty eligible employees with an average salary of $25,000, your total compensation is $1 million. Three percent of $1 million is $30,000. This assumes that (1) everyone participates, and (2) everyone contributes 6 percent of their pay. In most cases, not everyone will participate (American workers leave tens of billions of match money on the table every year) and not everyone will contribute to the full extent of the match. Therefore, it's generally safe to use a reduction factor of between 75 and 85 percent to get an accurate estimate of a company's real cost. Use a lower-percentage figure for a low-wage, high-turnover business and a higher-percentage figure for stable, high-wage industries. In our example, 80 percent of $30,000 is $24,000.

VESTING

Employer contributions may be subject to a "vesting" schedule, which refers to the "ownership" of employer contributions (employee contributions are always immediately vested.) There are many different ways to structure a vesting schedule.[5] Some schedules are "graded," i.e., they vest gradually over a period of years while others are "cliff," i.e., they vest all at once after a number of years.[6] For example, a plan with a three-year "cliff" vesting schedule means that employees with more than three years of service own all of the employer contributions made on their behalf. Employees with less than three years of service and those who terminate service cannot claim any of the contributions made on their behalf.

Vesting is a powerful tool to shape the retirement plan to help meet corporate objectives. For example, it can be used to combat high turnover and to keep employer costs low since people who quit prior to being 100-percent vested "forfeit" the money back to the plan.

✦   ✦   ✦

FORFEITURES

Employees who quit prior to becoming 100-percent vested in the employer contributions "forfeit" their unvested portion back to the plan. These monies are tracked separately from the employee and employer contributions. Each sponsor decides how to treat forfeitures. Here are some options:

+ Use forfeitures to offset administrative expenses of the plan.
+ Distribute the forfeitures back to the current plan participants.
+ Use forfeitures to pay for future employer contributions.

FINDING MONEY FOR AN EMPLOYER MATCH

Some companies, however, are not in a position to make a generous matching contribution. A cash-strapped company looking for ways to find contribution money should consider the following ideas:

+ Start with a modest discretionary 401(k) match; increase it over time.
+ Link it to a company-wide performance target like net profit[7].
+ Add a "last day" rule, i.e., an employee must be employed on the last day of the plan year to receive the employer-matching contribution.
+ Add a vesting schedule and use forfeitures to offset future employer contributions.
+ Consider reducing the profit-sharing or money-purchase contribution (if applicable) and use the savings for a 401(k) match.
+ Find savings in either another employee benefit plan (e.g., medical, dental, disability) or reduce annual merit increases to help pay for an employer contribution.
+ Shift a portion of the money earmarked for salary increases to fund a matching contribution: many workers prefer excellent retirement benefits over higher salaries[8].

A 401(k) matching contribution is key to a successful plan. It goes a long way to increasing participation and raising the savings percentage. There are different types of matching contributions and you should be able to select one to help you meet the needs of your company.

Notes

1. According to Fidelity data, 43 percent of plans offer an employer matching contribution of 2.1 to 3 percent. The majority of these have an effective match of exactly 3 percent. (43rd Annual Survey of Profit Sharing and 401(k) Plans, 1999.)

   The average company contribution was 4.7 percent of payroll. Company contributions were highest in profit-sharing plans (8.6 percent of payroll) and lowest in 401(k) plans (3.3 percent of payroll). Company contributions averaged 25.9 percent of total net profit for profit-sharing plans and 14.1 percent of total net profit for 401(k) plans.

   Numerous formulas are utilized to determine company contributions. In plans permitting participant contributions, the most common formula is a fixed match only, present in 30.6 percent of plans. The most common type of fixed match is $.50 per $1.00 up to the first 6 percent of pay, present in 25.1 percent of plans that have fixed matches. The most common type of company contribution for profit-sharing plans is a discretionary profit-sharing contribution only, which is present in 51.1 percent of plans.
   —(43rd Annual Survey of Profit Sharing and 401(k) Plans, 1999.)

2. "The Word Can Be Mightier Than the Match," Watson Wyatt Worldwide, 1996.

3. *Ibid.*

4. About 25 percent of 401(k) plans match contributions with company stock, according to Spectrem Group. "Fixes for a Broken 401(k) System," Karen Hube, MSN *MoneyCentral,* January 24, 2002.

5. Under the Tax Relief Act of 2001, for plan years beginning after 12/31/01, matching funds will be fully vested after the employee completes three years of service, instead of five years under the old law. Alternatively, employers can provide gradual vesting beginning with the employee's second year of service and ending after six years of service (compared to three to seven years under the old law.)

YEARS OF SERVICE	CLIFF VESTING		GRADUATED VESTING	
	Prior to 1/1/02	Beginning 1/1/02	Prior to 1/1/02	Beginning 1/1/02
0	0%	0%	0	0%
1	0%	0%	0	20%
2	0%	0%	20%	40%
3	0%	100%	30%	60%
4	0%		40%	80%
5	100%		60%	100%
6			80%	
7			100%	

6. "According to Mercer, over the last three years, 15% of the sample has liberalized the vesting requirement for the employer-matching contribution—driven primarily by the need to attract and retain qualified employees and the desire to stay competitive."

   + 37 percent of all plans report immediate vesting.
   + 46 percent have graded vesting.
   + The remainder have cliff vesting.

   "Eligibility, Vesting Requirements Getting Looser," *PlanSponsor.com,* December 27, 2001.

7. Research by Doug Kruse of Rutgers University shows that companies whose pay is linked to company profits by a specific percentage showed 6 to 7 percent productivity increases. "Yes, Profit Sharing Spurs Productivity, But Which Method Works Best?" Gene Epstein, *Barron's,* August 15, 1994.

8. "When asked whether they would prefer a job with excellent retirement benefits that meets their minimum salary requirements or a job with a higher salary but poor retirement benefits, full-time workers in companies with 10 to 500 employees tend to choose the excellent retirement benefits (57%) over the higher salary (36%). The preference for the excellent retirement benefits increases as workers age, but even among Generation X workers half prefer excellent retirement benefits (49%) to a higher salary (45%). Six in ten Baby Boomers (60%) and two thirds of pre-retirees (66%) also prefer the excellent benefits." Transamerica Retirement Survey 2001, Prepared by Mathew Greenwald & Associates, Inc., October 2001, p. 6.

PART

TWO

CHAPTER 7

401(K) ARCHITECTURE: BUILDING BLOCKS

✦

The first six chapters provided an overview of the 401(k) market-place, a survey of various retirement plans, a review of the legal underpinnings and government testing requirements, and design issues surrounding these plans. We now turn our attention to the discrete pieces that comprise every 401(k) plan, how they fit together, and how to evaluate each of these pieces in the buying process.

401(K) BUILDING BLOCKS

Every 401(k) plan is composed of five broad elements.

+ **Recordkeeping**—Links participants' accounts to the pooled investment selections by maintaining participants' account balances and records in the plan (e.g., valuing participant accounts, facilitating investment transfers, reconciling all records on specified dates and generating statements).

+ **Plan Administration**—This refers to the nuts-and-bolts operation of a plan, including payroll, tax compliance, implementation of participant-directed activity (e.g., loans, change of address, hardship withdrawals, etc.) and distribution processing.

+ **Investments**—This is the "engine" that drives account growth. The plan sponsor usually puts together a group of core investment options from which participants create their own investment mix. Service providers often use 401(k) plans as a platform from which to distribute their own "proprietary" investment product as well as to distribute other "nonproprietary" investment product.

+ **Legal Compliance**—Refers to the IRS and DOL regulations governing plans to ensure that the plan operates fairly with respect to all employees. The emphasis here is on the drafting, interpretation, and application of the legally required plan documents (e.g., plan document, trust agreement, adoption agreement, summary plan description, etc.) and annual discrimination testing and government reporting.

+ **Employee Education and Communication**—This is the ongoing effort to educate participants about the plan (e.g., how it operates, the benefits of pre-tax savings, withdrawal options, etc.) and about investments, so that informed decisions can be made.

The arrangement of these critical components influences the look and feel of the plan. Who performs these services, how these tasks are combined and how they are delivered creates the differences between the various products found in the 401(k) marketplace.

BASIC SERVICE DELIVERY MODELS: "UNBUNDLED," "BUNDLED," AND "ALLIANCE"

Below are the three main ways various service providers' products are structured. Please keep in mind that these definitions are not strict and that people use the terms loosely. However, they are useful in categorizing the different ways in which service providers position their products in the 401(k) marketplace.

+ **Unbundled**—The plan sponsor selects a separate organization to perform each critical task. The idea behind an unbundled plan is to get the best provider for each separate service. Since the service providers are not formally connected, responsibility for the coordination of the various tasks falls squarely on the plan sponsor's shoulders.

+ **Bundled**—The plan sponsor selects one organization that provides all recordkeeping, administration, trust, compliance, and investment services. The advantage to this one-stop-shopping model is that the plan sponsor has only one point of contact to handle the separate tasks. The term also suggests that the majority of the investments (if not all) will be the service provider's own proprietary investment products.

+ **Strategic Alliance**—Usually a variation of bundled, one vendor coordinates all services and quotes all fees. The key vendor in an alliance may outsource one or more critical functions to a strategic partner—usually investments and compliance. Alliances are often positioned as bundled arrangements, since coordination among vendors is usually transparent to the plan sponsor and participants.

Unbundled

Some plan sponsors want the freedom to pick the best service provider available for each of the essential services. This is how it would typically work for a large plan, the most common user of an unbundled arrangement.[1] The sponsor selects a stand-alone third-party administrator (TPA) or a large national consulting firm to provide recordkeeping and administration services. Compliance services are delegated to the law firm responsible for writing the plan document. The plan sponsor hires different money-management firms to provide investment services and seeks the lowest-cost version of their investment options. The plan sponsor's HR staff develops and executes employee communication and education materials, or outsources this task to a consulting firm. Finally, a third-party corporate trustee is hired to provide trust services. As you might guess, this type of arrangement is most often used by large companies with sufficient internal resources and by small professional organizations, which, because of the complexity of their plan design, are often required to use a third party administrator (TPA).

History

Large companies were the first to set up 401(k) plans in the early 1980s. Many of them also sponsored defined-benefit pension plans and trustee-directed profit-sharing plans.[2] Most of these traditional pension and profit-sharing plans were unbundled arrangements with separate companies providing recordkeeping, administration, actuarial, trust, and investment services. At that time, the recordkeeping requirements were usually limited to performing an annual valuation, sending out annual statements, and processing disbursements. Since the investments were generally selected and directed by the plan trustees, there was no need for ongoing employee education and communication. When large companies set up the first-generation 401(k) plans, it was only natural to use the same service-delivery model. Even if a company had wanted to, there were few, if any, bundled providers to choose from. As a result, most of the first-generation 401(k) plans were unbundled.

As the demand for more sophisticated 401(k) recordkeeping services grew (e.g., more frequent valuations, twenty-four-hour toll-free telephone access, greater investment flexibility, etc.), problems set in. These changing marketplace demands forced more frequent communication and coordination among separate providers; historically, something they were not accustomed to doing. The result was that the plan sponsor was forced to spend a lot of time and energy playing traffic cop between service providers. This lack of communication among the early market-share leaders (i.e., banks, insurance companies, and benefit-consulting firms) opened the way for bundled plans as plan sponsors looked for techno-logically enhanced, administratively simple plans to implement and run. Enter the large mutual fund companies.

Bundled

In a "bundled" plan, a single vendor performs most if not all of the crit-ical services. A vendor will sometimes outsource a service (usually annu-al testing and/or trust duties) to a strategic third-party partner, but will still market itself as a "one-stop shop" to clients and prospects. Most of the largest service providers today offer some kind of bundled package. These arrangements are now the overwhelming service delivery model of choice in the small and mid-market due to their convenience and repu-tation for low cost.[3] A typical bundled plan works like this.

The plan sponsor selects a bundled provider and uses the vendor's prototype plan document. The investments are selected from the service provider's menu of proprietary funds as well as from a pre-selected list of nonproprietary funds with which the bundled provider has a con-tractual arrangement to share investment revenue. The vendor provides recordkeeping services to plan participants, performs the annually required compliance tests, and usually completes Form 5500, the plan's tax return. Discretionary trustee services are provided either directly by the bundled provider's trust company or by a strategic partner.

History

The no-load mutual fund companies like Fidelity, Dreyfus, Vanguard, and T. Rowe Price revolutionized the 401(k) marketplace. In the late 1970s and early 1980s, with interest rates sky-high, Americans in large numbers began to transfer money from their low-yielding bank savings accounts to higher yielding money-market funds. As the 1982 recession ended and the great 1980s bull market began, more Americans shifted their financial assets to stock-and-bond mutual funds. These same investors began to demand that their companies' 401(k)s look and feel like their personal mutual fund accounts, with toll-free telephone tech-nology, daily valuations, and quarterly statements. By concentrating on the individual or "retail" investor and supporting him with state-of-the-art technology and high levels of customer service, fund companies raised the competitive benchmark for the entire financial services industry, including qualified retirement plans. Companies began to look to the large mutual fund houses as 401(k) service providers, and the mutual fund houses were only too happy to oblige.[4]

During the late 1980s, the mutual fund companies began full-service bundled 401(k) operations as a means to efficiently gather assets. The large fund families used the fees generated from their fast-growing proprietary funds to subsidize the explicit recordkeeping costs. This made them appear to be less expensive than a typical unbundled arrangement. With their technology, lower explicit costs, and one-stop-shop marketing sales pitches, the bundled providers quickly gained market share at the expense of unbundled providers.

The first-generation bundled plans came at a price, however. What plan sponsors gained in simplicity, sophisticated technology, and lower administrative costs, they gave up in investment flexibility. First-generation bundled providers required that plan sponsors use their proprietary investments almost exclusively. As the 1990s began, participants started to demand greater access to multimanager fund choices. Enter the alliances.

Alliance Platform

The third type of 401(k) service delivery model is called the "alliance" system. This approach combines features of both bundled and unbundled plans and has exploded in popularity.[5] In an alliance model, a plan sponsor contracts with a single service provider who provides recordkeeping and administration, compliance, and education services, just like a bundled provider. Investment options, however, are greatly expanded. In addition to selecting from the service provider's list of proprietary investment options, a typical alliance product allows a sponsor to choose some investments from a vendor's nonproprietary investment universe. The usual stipulation is that either a minimum percentage of assets or a certain number of the investment options must go into the vendor's own proprietary investments. In order to explain how the alliance platform works in more detail, it is helpful to see how it got started.

Charles Schwab's Revolutionary Idea

In 1993, Charles Schwab started the Schwab OneSource program allowing investors to select from a supermarket of over 200 mutual funds. The idea was simple. Instead of "manufacturing" investment product and competing against the traditional investment management firms like American Funds, Fidelity, Putnam, and Vanguard, Schwab instead would distribute other companies' investment product and receive a small fee for the service. It was an idea whose time had come, and today mutual fund "supermarkets," as they are now known, are everywhere. Today, Schwab's OneSource offers over 3,500 funds from over 200 fund families, and other companies like Waterhouse Securities, Fidelity, and E∗Trade have created their own mutual fund supermarkets. The alliance concept was also quickly embraced by employee benefits consulting firms like Hewitt in the large plan marketplace. To protect their traditional 401(k) recordkeeping business against bundled mutual fund providers, they formed strategic alliances with smaller fund families that lacked defined contribution recordkeeping and administrative capabilities. As more and more 401(k) vendors adopted the alliance concept, more and more plan sponsors and participants demanded the ability to access multiple fund families from a single source. Here's how a typical alliance product works.

The plan sponsor selects from a predetermined universe consisting of the service provider's proprietary funds as well as a select number of nonproprietary "outside" funds. To protect its profit margins (proprietary investments generate more revenue than nonproprietary ones), the alliance provider usually requires that a minimum percentage of assets flow into their funds, or a minimum number of proprietary funds be used. The nonproprietary, or "outside," funds pay the alliance provider a distribution fee in the form of a 12b-1 and/or sub-transfer agent fees.[6] This common industry practice is known as "revenue sharing."

In effect, the alliance provider is being paid to distribute someone else's product. If a fund is truly "no-load" and is not designed for revenue sharing, then the alliance provider will usually charge an asset-based fee in order to reimburse itself for the cost of distribution. (See chapter 11, "Plan Costs," for a more detailed discussion of mutual fund pricing.)

The alliance model's new twist is the 12b-1 rebate. The result is that alliance products can offer the same pricing structure as a bundled product without restricting investment choices to one fund family. (This assumes that the plan's total assets and average participant account balances are sufficiently large.) Due to the rapid growth of the alliance model, there are many alliance products in the market today even for small plans.[7]

The table below briefly summarizes the differences between the three main models.

TABLE 1:
401(K) ARCHITECTURE—ADVANTAGES AND DISADVANTAGES

	Unbundled	Bundled	Alliance
Administrative Ease	Multiple Contact Points	Single Contact Point	Single Contact Point
Investment Flexibility	High	Low to Medium	Medium to High
Record-keeping Costs	High	Low (record-keeping costs offset by investment fees)	Low (record-keeping costs offset by investment fees)
Investment Costs	Low	Low to medium	Medium to high (limited to revenue sharing funds)
Flexibility to Select the "Best of the Best"	Yes	None to very limited	None to very limited
Integrated Record-keeping & Technology Platform	Low to medium	Medium to high	Medium to high
Participant Education	Custom to semi-custom	Off the Shelf to semi-custom	Off the Shelf to semi-custom
Plan Sponsor Involvement	Medium to high	Low to medium	Low to medium

THE IMPORTANCE OF 401(K) ARCHITECTURE

When you understand the different ways in which plans can be assembled, it becomes easier to quickly categorize various products and to understand the inherent tradeoffs within and between each model. Ultimately, this makes you a better shopper. Deciding on the proper service delivery model for your company can dramatically affect your workload and the way services are delivered. And although there is no right or wrong way, market statistics and trends show that the de facto industry standard for the majority of plans is the bundled alliance product. In the end, decisions about how to structure your plan should be specific to your company. As you read the next several chapters about each of the component pieces, such as recordkeeping and administration, investments, and employee education and communication, keep in mind how these parts will fit into the whole. Some questions to ask yourself as you consider various 401(k) service delivery models include:

+ How many internal resources can you commit to the operation of a plan?
+ Does the company usually outsource nonessential business tasks or does it do everything in-house?
+ What are the goals of the plan: Maximum investment flexibility? Lowest explicit costs? The ability to outsource the plan?
+ How do you value the trade-off between lower administrative fees at the expense of possibly higher investment management fees?
+ If you have a plan already, does the current architecture help or hurt the plan?
+ What levels of service do you require? How does each arrangement meet these requirements?
+ What are the needs of the participants for reporting, technology interface features, and employee education and communication?
+ How complex is the plan's design? Does it require you to use a specialized TPA?

Notes

1. Source: Speech made by a Consultant from Cerulli Associates, Inc. at the Scudder Investments Consultant Symposium held on February 1, 2002 in Key Biscayne, FL—Slide 26

   Cerulli Associates, Sanford Bernstein, DOL, CFO Magazine, Pensions & Investments, Plan Sponsor Magazine

2. In a trustee-directed plan, the trustees select the investments for the plan and invest the money for all of the participants. In a participant-directed plan, the overwhelmingly used model today, the trustee selects the investments but the participant directs her investment selections.

3. "Bundled services are most prevalent among small and medium sized plans. According to one study, among plans with fewer than 250 participants, 85 percent rely on bundled services; among plans with from 250–1,000 participants, about 75% use this product (Fink)."

   "How is the Administration of 401(k) Plans Structured?"

   http://401k-administration.com/administration.html

4. The ten largest firms run about 72% of the $2.4 trillion in assets under recordkeeping by the firms surveyed, the survey indicated. Those ten—from the most to the least—are Fidelity, TIAA-CREF, CitiStreet, Hewitt, Merrill Lynch, Vanguard, MetLife, Inc., Putnam, T. Rowe Price, and Aetna, which recently sold its retirement business to ING.

   Overall, Fidelity Investments, Boston, is in the top slot this year, recordkeeping the most assets, $480 billion, and participants, 8.3 million. The Teachers Insurance and Annuity Association, New York, ranked second in assets, with $295 billion, and eighth in terms of number of participants, with 2.3 million. Newcomer CitiStreet, Boston, ranked third in terms of both assets, $200 billion, and number of participant account records kept, 5.4 million. Hewitt Associates LLC, the only recordkeeper in the top ten without a line of proprietary funds, was fourth in assets records kept with $180 billion, and second in number of participants with 4.5 million.

   "10 Firms Dominate Recordkeeping," Arlene Jacobius, "Pensions & Investments," October 2, 2000.

5. Percentage of plans offering funds managed by mulitple investment managers:

- ✦ Under $5 million: 54.6%
- ✦ $5–50 million: 66.6%
- ✦ $50–200 million: $74.3%
- ✦ $200–500 million: 82.%
- ✦ $500 million plus: 82.7%

"2001 DC Survey," *PlanSponsor Magazine*, November 2001, p. 50

6. 12b-1 fees are used to finance fund distribution. They are part of a fund's total expense ratio and are usually between 25 and 75 basis points (0.25%–0.75%).

7. *Op cit*, note 3.

CHAPTER 8

RECORDKEEPING/
ADMINISTRATION AND PLAN
TECHNOLOGY

◆

As a 401(k) buyer, you want to get the best value you and your employees' money can buy. Error-free recordkeeping, top-notch administration and enabling technology comprise the bedrock of a good plan and the minimum baseline criteria for vendor selection. Record-keeping and other supporting technology will go a long way in determining how your employees perceive the plan as well as how much time and effort you put into administering the plan. When supported by powerful technology systems, recordkeeping can minimize or even eliminate many of the time-consuming chores often associated with retirement plan administration. This chapter will look at 401(k) recordkeeping, what it is, its evolution over the past twenty years, and where it's headed. Finally, I will list the questions you need to ask your current or prospective recordkeeping provider.

WHAT IS RECORDKEEPING?

In its simplest form, recordkeeping refers to the tracking of employer and employee contributions and the calculation of investment gains and losses and dividend distributions. Today, recordkeeping has also come to mean not only the tracking of investment gains and losses, directing distributions, and determining plan enforcement issues (e.g., eligibility, vesting, hardship, etc.), but also the complementary technology systems supporting the delivery of plan information to both plan participants and sponsors. This includes daily valuation, toll-free interactive voice response, customer-service call centers, and a full suite of online services.

Like most good things we take for granted, most people only notice good recordkeeping when it breaks down and headaches occur. Tracking investments and contributions across multiple investment options may not seem like much, but the underlying systems supporting such intricate operations are quite complex. Valuation frequency, participant records, number and kind of investment vehicles, and plan design complexity (e.g., employer contributions including match and profit sharing, vesting, forfeitures, loans, post-tax deferrals, etc.) all must be accounted for. Recordkeeping is one of those essential but thankless jobs; you know things are working well when no one talks about it. Let's take a moment and look at the evolution of 401(k) recordkeeping.

First-Generation Recordkeeping

When 401(k) plans started in the early 1980s, recordkeeping was a simple affair. First-generation 401(k) plans were handled by banks, insurance companies, and third-party administrators (TPAs), including large consulting firms. Many of these firms had their roots in pooled trust accounts and defined benefit plans where assets were valued once a year. In these early plans, the trustees would often direct the investments for the participants. If everything went well, a participant would receive his annual 401(k) or profit-sharing statement two to six months after the end of the plan year. By the time the participant received it, the statement was already dated, since it could take a plan administrator weeks or even months to perform the calculation for a single plan.

THE RISE OF THE MUTUAL FUNDS AND DAILY VALUATION

This all began to change by the mid-1980s with the growing popularity of mutual funds. Taking advantage of the increased power and lower cost of computers, mutual fund companies began to gobble up market share from the traditional pension providers—banks and insurance companies. The expectations of 401(k) participants who already had personal accounts with retail fund companies began to change as they appreciated the mutual fund industry's standard offering of daily valuation, participant-directed investment choices, and toll-free telephone access. People who were used to the convenience of speaking to mutual fund customer-service representatives about their own personal accounts and who were used to moving money between their own investment options on a daily basis, began to demand the same conveniences from their 401(k) plans. Banks, insurance companies, TPAs and other service providers rushed to move their recordkeeping systems into the world of daily valuation and advanced plan features, changing the entire retirement industry in the process.[1]

MAINSTREAMING OF ADVANCED PLAN TECHNOLOGY

Over the past decade, technology has reshaped the retirement plan business. Features that a few years ago were considered cutting edge, are now mainstream. The leading service providers have invested millions of dollars to upgrade their recordkeeping systems, thereby enabling participant access to real-time information and removing the plan sponsor from the majority of day-to-day participant transactions. The ideas underpinning these new technology systems are employee "self-service" and "outsourcing"—allowing participants to access accurate personal and plan information across multiple media whenever they choose, with no involvement from the sponsor required.

Participants can now direct their multi-fund and multi-fund family investment options twenty-four hours a day over the phone or the Internet, through a single recordkeeping platform. Today, participants can access an interactive voice response (IVR) system, the Internet, or a customer-service center to complete most 401(k) plan–related inquiries and transactions. The daily valued, twenty-four-hour toll-free access, participant- directed 401(k) plan has become the de facto industry standard and a minimum competitive benchmark for service providers.[2] We now turn our attention to the understanding and evaluation of the pieces that comprise these systems.

CORE RECORDKEEPING SYSTEM

Many large service providers use either Sunguard's Omniplus system or the Trustmark platform for recordkeeping. Some providers have bought the systems outright, extensively configuring them so that they become their own proprietary systems while others rent them, paying an annual leasing fee that covers maintenance and upgrade costs of these constantly evolving systems. Both systems are PC-based and Windows-compatible.

Some full-service bundled providers have developed their own proprietary systems. Usually, these are mainframe "legacy" systems that were originally used by the service provider in their traditional pension business and have been modified to accommodate increasing plan-design and investment complexity.

Almost all recordkeeping systems are daily valued, which means that participants' accounts are updated based on that day's closing market prices. Daily valuation allows participants to continually monitor the value of their account and to make changes to it on a daily basis. As long as investment changes are executed prior to the market's closing, orders are processed the same day.

INTERACTIVE VOICE RESPONSE (IVR)

The IVR system offers participants access to their account and the information it contains. At a minimum, a good IVR system should allow participants to complete the following transactions:

- ✦ Account balance inquiries
- ✦ Investment election changes
- ✦ Transfers of balances between investment options
- ✦ Contribution rate changes
- ✦ Loan modeling and processing
- ✦ Benefit distribution initiation

CALL CENTER

Although useful, an IVR system is static. If a participant wants to talk to a real person, they opt out to a call center. At a minimum, good call centers maintain long hours and are usually staffed by licensed investment professionals who answer their phones quickly, with the help of intelligent call-routing software. The best call centers also track participant calls and use technology that quickly "pops up" participant account information when transferring a call from the IVR. This also includes access to "imaged" documents, so that the representative can look at electronic versions of paper documents, eliminating the need to keep huge paper files nearby and saving valuable time. In addition, the best call centers hire friendly and personable people, train and retrain their representatives, compensate them well, offer opportunities for career growth, and develop customized scripts for answering difficult, plan-specific questions. Finally, world-class call centers have each client's plan rules "hard wired" into the recordkeeping system to minimize human error and prevent costly mistakes.

ONLINE SERVICES

Over half of all Americans are connected to the Internet, either at work or at home.[3] The Internet has had a profound impact on the retirement industry, from the way participants and plan sponsors access information to the way plans are distributed.[4] The Internet can provide participants with timely, consistent, and accurate information about their benefit plans. It is also an excellent medium for both sponsor and participant to access data or execute routine transactions.

Whatever a participant can do through the IVR, she should be able to do through the Internet. The real power of the Internet is its ability to effectively provide detailed and personalized information anyplace, anytime. For example, asset-allocation software, retirement-projection tools, and historical-investment information can be easily provided through this dynamic medium.

From the sponsor's perspective, the value of the Internet is twofold. First, it allows sponsors to quickly and efficiently transmit payroll information. This basic task, sending a contribution file every two weeks, for example, is a critical function. With participants closely watching their money, this allows their contributions to be posted faster and with fewer mistakes.[5] Second, the Internet allows sponsors to easily look at reports and assess the overall condition of their plan. Rather than rely on a recordkeeper's quarterly trust reports, sponsors can check a plan's participation, savings percentage, and asset allocation by various age, sex, and income levels in real time. The power of immediate access to key information also allows plan sponsors to be proactive and targeted in their education and communication efforts.

DISTINGUISHING AMONG RECORDKEEPERS

At first blush, it appears difficult to distinguish among the many recordkeepers available today. Since most plans are both daily valued and participant-directed, I will restrict my comments to this standard and exclude any recordkeepers who do not provide this service.

The first step is understanding your recordkeeping and administrative requirements, which, in turn, requires calculating your present and future plan design and operational needs. How many participants are in your plan? How many transactions does your staff get involved in (enrollments, loans, hardship distributions, terminations, statements, etc.)? Who is going to prepare the legally required documents, perform annual discrimination tests and submit regular government filings (e.g., SPD's, ADP/ACP tests, 5500's, 1099-R's, etc.)? Could you effectively turn these administrative duties over to someone else? Answering the following questions should help you to winnow out high-quality record-keeping candidates. (We discuss the use of a Request for Proposal during the vendor-search process in chapter 13.)

- How many plans and participants does the recordkeeper support?
- Are current clients satisfied?
- Did any ex-clients leave because of operational issues?
- Can it accommodate all of your current plan-design features? Can it competently consult on alternative plan designs?
- Is the system audited to ensure accurate operational procedures?
- How much money does the recordkeeper earmark annually for system maintenance and enhancements?
- How does the system interface with your payroll system?
- Are all of the administrative procedures adequately described in an easy-to-use administrative manual?
- Does the vendor offer service standards for basic transactions (e.g., loans, distributions, statements)? What are they and how do they compare to the competition?
- Does it back them up with performance-based guarantees? What are they and how do they compare to the competition?
- What kind of report generation capability does it have? Standard reports? Ad hoc?
- Does the recordkeeper perform all compliance tests needed to maintain the plan's qualified status? Does it outsource any of these tasks to a third party?
- Does the recordkeeper prepare and file all required government filings needed to maintain the plan's qualified status (e.g., SPD, W-2, 1099-R, 5500)?
- Does it have any inherent limitations about the number or kind of investment options? Can it maintain your company stock?

+ Does the participant have online access to his account? Is it fully transactional?
+ Does the sponsor have online access to aggregate plan data? Can the sponsor generate ad hoc reports?
+ Is the core recordkeeping system fully integrated with the IVR and Internet?
+ Can participants model and initiate loans by telephone?
+ Does the IVR system allow for Internet and telephone-based enrollments?
+ If there are questions about recordkeeping or administrative functions, can the sponsor speak to a dedicated account executive?

Notes

1. Today, almost all new plans and about 90 percent of all plans are daily valued.

2. The use of voice-response systems has grown dramatically over the past several years. Voice-response systems are used by 85 percent of respondents in this year's survey, up from 35 percent in our 1993 survey. (401(k) Plans Survey Report on Plan Design, 1998 Plan Year, Buck Consultants, p. 3.)

   The percentage of plans performing daily valuation of fund balances continues to rise, reaching 89 percent this year, up from 71 percent in 1997. (Trends & Experience in 401(k) Plans, Hewitt Associates, 1999.)

3. As of November 2000, 55.83 percent or 153.84 million Americans were online. *www.nua.net/surveys.*

4. "Plan participants now have access to their 401(k) through the Internet in 82% of the plans surveyed. Of these plans, 90% offer transactional capabilities." Morgan Stanley Dean Witter Investment Management 2000 Survey of the 401(k) Market.

5. After an employee's 401(k) plan elective deferrals are withheld from the employee's paycheck, the deferrals become plan assets on the earliest date on which such

contributions can reasonably be segregated from the employer's general assets. DOL Reg. Sec. 2510-102(a). The DOL regulations furthur provide that in no event may the date of deposit be later than the 15th business day of the month following the month in which the amounts would have been payable to the participant in cash. DOL Reg. Sec. 2510-102(b).

CHAPTER 9

INVESTMENTS

✦

Investments are the backbone of any good retirement plan. In participant-directed plans like 401(k), the care and attention devoted to investment decisions cannot be overstated.[1] Selecting and monitoring investment options whether they come bundled, as part of an alliance, or completely unbundled, are some of a plan sponsor's main fiduciary responsibilities.[2]

This chapter is about investments and the key things you need to know about designing, selecting, and monitoring an investment portfolio while protecting yourself from participant-driven lawsuits. After reading this chapter, you should have enough information to research, organize, and evaluate the different investments your current or prospective provider offers you.

Sound investment decisions are even more relevant in light of the bear market of the past couple of years and the recent dot-com meltdown. Ironically, people pay more attention to their investment portfolio in a down or lackluster market environment. Today's high average account balances coupled with a bear market mean people have more at stake and more to lose. As we saw in chapter 3, "Fiduciary Responsibility," the investment selection and monitoring process is expected to become a legal battleground as the great tide of baby boomers retires.

STOCK MARKET NATION

The number and kind of investment products has exploded in the past twenty years. There are now over seven thousand actively traded stocks in the United States and over twelve thousand retail mutual funds.[3] In addition, there are thousands of other investment vehicles, such as collective trusts, separate accounts, variable annuities, and private money managers. There are small, medium, and large cap stocks, government and corporate bonds of short, intermediate, and long duration, as well as guaranteed investment contracts and real estate trusts.

This exploding investment universe has dramatically changed the 401(k) marketplace. Only a few years ago, plan sponsors might have selected from a total investment universe of twenty to fifty options. Today, plan sponsors routinely select from fifty, five hundred, and even a thousand available investment options. Not surprisingly, the number of investment options offered to participants continues to grow as well. This trend toward investment choice will continue to grow—fueled in large part by the increasing role of fund supermarkets like Charles Schwab. More choice is usually a good thing, but in the case of 401(k) plans, making sense of the vast investment universe can seem overwhelming for participant and sponsor alike.

INVESTMENT POLICY STATEMENT (IPS)

It doesn't matter if you are a start-up plan or already have an established program; a well-designed IPS is an important fiduciary tool. A well-written IPS is an essential tool for understanding the investment universe and protecting you and your company at the same time. Just as a good financial advisor would never dream of recommending an investment without first understanding your goals and risk tolerance, selecting investments without first considering employee demographics, the number and kind of investment options, and risk-adjusted performance and costs, is now unthinkable. In the investment world, knowing what you don't want or need is just as important as knowing what you do. A well-drafted IPS helps to establish a logical, coherent framework for the development and adherence of corporate retirement plan investment goals.

There are many benefits that accrue to a company by establishing an IPS. First, it's a written document. The act of sitting down and writing forces a plan sponsor to think through investment decisions while documenting the rationale. By committing decisions to paper, an IPS eliminates secondguessing by making clear the investment selection and monitoring criteria. As the company changes, a chronicle of why decisions were made, an investment history, is left behind. Finally, a well-written IPS also provides a baseline for the ongoing monitoring of investments. When so many 401(k) vendors are offering increased investment choices, having a compass by which to guide the investment selection process is absolutely necessary.

Legal Basis for an IPS

In addition to the practical reasons for writing an IPS, there are legal reasons as well. ERISA requires that all plans have a well-defined funding policy. Post-ERISA case law, DOL releases, industry practice, and growing participant-account balances make the adoption of an IPS a virtual necessity. The spirit of ERISA in this regard is to force plan-sponsor process and discipline. The hallmark of all successful investors is that they develop clear investment goals and strategies and stick to them over time. A well-designed IPS will prevent the plan sponsor from making ill-advised investment selections not only at inception, but throughout the life of the plan. Finally, if you were ever to be sued by a plan participant, an up-to-date working IPS demonstrates procedural process.

Building an IPS: Group Demographics

The easiest way to begin to construct an IPS is to define the workforce. Are the employees younger or older, on average? Are the employees knowledgeable about investments? Have they had a retirement plan before, or is this their first one? What is the average income, estimated account balance, and what percentage of employees will participate across various income levels? Getting a handle on the group's demographics will lead to a better understanding of which investment options to include.

THE STRUCTURE OF AN IPS

The structure of an IPS is simple. It describes the company, the investment selection and monitoring process, and the reasons specific investments are included. A well-written IPS defines the objectives of the plan, the asset classes to be included, the decision-making committee members, and sets forth the criteria to be used in the selection and monitoring process. A good IPS generally addresses the following issues:

+ **Mission Statement**—This explains why the plan exists, group demographics (e.g., age, income, education, etc.), whether it is participant or trustee-directed, and whether it intends to comply with 404(c).

+ **Asset Allocation**—What asset classes should be included to allow participants to achieve optimal asset allocation? Which ones are not necessary?

+ **Investment Objectives**—What kind of return is acceptable? What benchmarks will be used to evaluate investments both initially and on an ongoing basis?

+ **Risk Tolerance**—How much risk is the plan willing to let participants take? For example, do you include speculative investments or a fund that makes a large sector bet?

+ **Review Procedures**—An IPS is a living document. A well-written one lays out the criteria for monitoring and the removal of poorly performing funds. The plan must be periodically reviewed to ensure that it is on track.

The key to a successful investment program is having a well-defined IPS based on your company specifics. Unfortunately, many sponsors, particularly of small plans, spend too little time selecting their investments and even less time monitoring the results. More often than not, companies delegate this responsibility to the salesperson, or even worse, consult a "top ten" fund list. As participant account balances grow, this laissez-faire approach will become increasingly risky. It leaves sponsors open to lawsuits from "aggrieved" participants claiming that because the sponsor did not use a formal process in reviewing, selecting, and monitoring investments, they were subject to poorly performing funds which prevented them from achieving retirement security. A meaningful IPS is an effective tool that will serve as a first line of defense against those kinds of charges.

WHICH INVESTMENT VEHICLES TO USE IN A 401(K) PLAN

ERISA only explicitly prohibits collectibles and large personal property as investment vehicles for 401(k) plans. Plan sponsors are free to select from the following list of investments:

+ Mutual funds
+ Insurance and annuity contracts
+ Bank commingled trusts and deposits
+ Stocks, bonds, and government securities
+ Partnerships, real estate, mortgages
+ Options, futures, and commodities

ERISA requires that fiduciaries diversify plan investments when necessary to minimize the risk of large losses.[4] Therefore, the prevailing practice today is to use diversified and highly liquid investment vehicles. For most plans, this means that the choices are annuity contracts, commingled trusts, and, most important of all, mutual funds.

THE COIN OF THE 401(K) REALM: MUTUAL FUNDS

Retail mutual funds have become the dominant investment vehicle of choice in 401(k) plans. One of their most appealing traits is simplicity. A mutual fund pools money from many investors and invests it on the basis of a clearly stated objective. Some invest primarily in stocks, some in bonds, and some in combination. In exchange for their services, they charge a fee based on a percentage of assets known as the expense ratio.

The reason for their popularity is simple—these investments are liquid, highly visible (i.e., they trade on a daily basis and can be easily looked up in the newspaper), and, because many retail fund families spend heavily on advertising, they are familiar to participants.

There are several advantages to using mutual funds.[5] First, owning many individual securities allows individuals to get instant diversification. This eliminates the risk of putting too many eggs in one basket and provides a cushion when markets fall. Second, mutual funds also offer the advantage of professional management, which in bear markets can often reduce risk and volatility.[6] Third, mutual funds are liquid and easy to buy. Because they trade regularly, participants can buy and sell shares on a daily basis. And since most mutual funds have modest minimum account purchase requirements, they are perfect for the weekly, biweekly, and monthly flow of most plans. Finally, because mutual funds are registered with the Securities Exchange Commission (SEC), they must disclose key operational information about themselves in a critical legal document, the prospectus.

As I mentioned earlier, there are now more than twelve thousand mutual funds—far more than the number of stocks listed on the NYSE. Many of the larger fund families, such as Fidelity[7] and Vanguard, sell directly to individuals, while many others, like American Funds, Putnam, and MFS, distribute their products through financial advisor networks. Either way, each of these companies has spent millions to create a corporate image and brand-name recognition[8]—a necessity in the hypercompetitive world of mutual-fund marketing. As a result, many employers feel comfortable giving their employees access to only name-brand, retail mutual funds whose prices they can track in the daily newspaper.

VARIATIONS ON MUTUAL FUNDS: ANNUITY CONTRACTS AND COLLECTIVE TRUSTS

Many insurance companies also use brand-name mutual funds as investment options within their 401(k) products. The underlying fund is wrapped in an insurance company's group variable annuity shell for legal and marketing purposes. Unlike mutual funds, these investment vehicles are not required to be registered with the SEC. This allows the insurance companies to sell their product through their traditional distribution channel—insurance agents and employee benefit brokers—many of whom are not securities-licensed to sell registered products. These investments are often marketed as if they were the actual mutual funds. Although similar, annuity contracts are almost always more expensive than the underlying mutual fund because of the additional asset-based fees they tack on. A portion of this additional fee is usually paid to the broker as a commission for selling the product, and the rest is used to subsidize plan costs and to keep the billed expenses low. Since the plans that buy them, start-up and small plans, lack enough total plan assets to offset the true cost of the plan, the service provider imposes the fee as an additional source of revenue. We will discuss this topic in more detail in chapter 11, "Plan Costs."

SEPARATE ACCOUNTS AND COMMINGLED TRUST FUNDS

Before mutual funds became the dominant 401(k) investment vehicle, separate accounts and collective, or commingled trusts were common.

A separate account is a customized portfolio designed to meet the needs of a particular investor or group of investors. Since these funds are not registered with the SEC nor marketed to the public, their cost is usually less than a retail mutual fund.

A collective trust fund is an investment vehicle created by pooling assets of unrelated retirement plans. They are most often managed by the trust departments of banks. Just like a separate account or annuity contract, these funds are not registered with the SEC nor marketed to the general public, and consequently their cost structure is generally less than a retail mutual fund.

Both of these types of investment vehicles are regaining their popularity due to the pricing advantage they often maintain over retail funds. However, there are disadvantages. Since neither of these vehicles are sold to the general public, and since they are not registered with the SEC, they lack the transparency and name brand caché of highly regulated mutual funds. For participants, this means that it can be difficult to get detailed information about them. We now turn our attention away from investment products to a discussion of the fund selection process and key selection criteria.

DESIGNING A PORTFOLIO: ASSET CLASSES AS BUILDING BLOCKS

Many plan sponsors pick individual "hot" funds rather than design a well thought-out portfolio. The difference is more than semantic. Starting with assets classes rather than the "best" funds is the first step in designing a sound investment strategy. At a minimum, most plans will include three core options: cash, bonds, and stock. Using these three investment options should enable the participants to devise a sufficiently diversified portfolio to achieve their objectives. In addition, offering three materially different options partially protects the plan sponsor from poor investment-performance claims under the guise of 404(c) regulations. I discuss this topic in more detail in chapter 3, "Fiduciary Responsibility," and chapter 10, "Employee Communication, Education, and Investment Advice."

REFINING CORE ASSET CLASSES

As you settle on the core asset classes you want represented, the process of refining becomes more complex. Do you include a money market fund, a fixed guaranteed account, or both? How many total funds do you offer? Do you include a short-term bond fund if you already have a guaranteed account? Defining and refining asset classes takes time and forces the decision-maker to consider for whom the investments are intended and how they will be used. Also, the need to create meaningful distinctions among asset classes must be weighed against the increased difficulty in communicating investment choices to employees. Too many fund options can lead to participant overload and confusion.

THE IMPORTANCE OF INVESTMENT STYLES

In addition to core asset classes, there are also various investment styles to consider when building a core portfolio. Including different styles should enable an investor to create a truly diversified portfolio.

- **Value and Growth**—Value and Growth styles are the yin and yang of investing. Value investors search out underperforming and out-of-favor companies (relative to the market) whose core business still remains operationally sound. Growth investors, on the other hand, seek companies whose earnings, sales, margins, and stock price are growing rapidly.

- **International and Domestic**—Although the United States is the world's largest economy, there are many attractive companies in other countries. Investing outside the United States allows investors to further diversify their portfolio.

- **Market Capitalization**—Companies of different sizes exhibit different patterns of growth. Generally speaking, companies with market capitalizations greater than $20 billion form the corporate elite. Midsize companies range between $2 billion and $20 billion of market capitalization. Small caps are companies with market capitalizations of between $250 million and $2 billion.[9] General economic conditions affect all companies, but the stock prices of large, medium, and small companies do not move in tandem, and in fact may tend to move countercyclically. When one group goes up, another one may go down, and vice versa. As a result, astute investors create portfolios with companies of different sizes in order to reduce risk.

+ **Active and Passive (Index)**—Indexing began as an academic thesis in the early 1970s and has since transformed the pension industry.[10] Unlike an actively managed portfolio, which fundamentally assumes that some stocks are under- or overvalued relative to others, a passively managed portfolio seeks to replicate an index like the S&P 500, Russell 2000, or Wilshire 5000. Because indexed portfolios do not have to support the research infrastructure of an actively managed portfolio, their cost is significantly lower. Index funds also have lower turnover ratios and as a result have lower overall transaction costs. This lower-cost structure makes them an excellent option for a qualified plan.

+ **Self-Directed Brokerage Account (SDBA)**—Although SDBAs are not an asset class per se, I include them here because of their special features. A SDBA allows a participant to buy individual securities like stocks and bonds as well as mutual funds that fall outside of the core investment lineup. As a plan sponsor, you have to make a decision as to whether or not they will do more harm than good for your population. Although virtually all the major 401(k) providers now offer SDBAs, few participants actually use them.[11] Yet for the person who knows what she is doing, a brokerage account can be an excellent way to control one's portfolio and enhance one's returns.

+ **Company Stock**—As noted earlier in chapter 6, offering company stock either as a stand-alone investment option or as the basis of the employer-matching contribution, is common in many large company 401(k) plans.[12] I strongly recommend against company stock as a stand-alone investment option except for the largest companies. The fiduciary and operational issues associated with offering company stock in a small or mid-size plan are significant and in light of the Enron and Global Crossing debacles, are best left alone.[13]

Participants often feel an emotional tug to buy company stock despite the risk of over-concentrating their retirement assets. On the other hand, buying company stock in the 401(k) plan gives participants a chance to own shares in the company and to strengthen the relationship between individual and company performance. A workable compromise is to allow participants who receive matching contributions in the form of company stock the option of moving out of the company stock within a reasonable period of time, and to voluntarily limit the amount a participant can invest in, to say, 25 percent. In addition, participants need to be educated about the inherent riskiness of owning an individual security as opposed to a diversified basket of stocks and bonds.

PUTTING IT ALL TOGETHER: FUND SELECTION CRITERIA AND PROCESS

Putting together a well-designed portfolio to meet your participants' needs cannot be reduced to a simple formula. It comes down to doing your homework, using reliable data, making informed choices, and, hopefully, documenting the process. You have to protect yourself when selecting funds. The way you conduct the process speaks volumes about your commitment to your plan and to overall procedural due diligence—two important considerations should you ever find yourself facing a participant lawsuit. If the task seems too daunting, hire a third-party investment consultant to help guide you through the process.[14]

There are several criteria to consider when selecting funds. Typically, these criteria are outlined in the IPS, so that the plan has a reference point with which to evaluate funds and performance over time.

+ **Annualized Investment Performance Over 1-, 3-, 5-, and 10-Year Periods**—Investment performance net of all fees is the starting point of historical analysis. This includes both calendar year and annualized information over a number of years. Ideally, investments should have a minimum three-year track record.

+ **Risk-adjusted Performance over 1-, 3-, 5-, and 10-Year Intervals**—The best measurement of investment performance is risk-adjusted returns, since it levels the playing field by handicapping the gross returns by the amount of "risk" taken to achieve those returns. Those with the least risk per unit of return are better, by definition. Risk is defined here by the fund's volatility (standard deviation) or by its performance relative to the market (beta). Another risk metric includes investment performance during a down market. This is referred to as "downside" risk.

+ **Peer Group (Category) and Comparative Index Performance**—Funds have different objectives and invest in different types of securities. It doesn't make sense to compare a small-cap value fund to a large-cap growth fund. How does the fund's performance compare to its best-fit index, and how does the fund's performance stack up against similar funds? These comparisons also help put performance numbers into context. Although a particular category like small cap or international stock may have had a bad year and lost money, your fund may have performed well within its category.

+ **Expenses**—This includes operating expenses, management fees, 12b-1 fees, sub-transfer agent fees, and all other asset-based costs. It is commonly accepted that fund expense is a key determinant of long-term historical performance. The higher the fund's expense, generally speaking, the less likely the fund will perform well. If possible, try to get "institutionally" priced investment options, as these are lower-cost versions of their more expensive "retail" cousins. We will discuss fund pricing in more detail in chapter 11, "Plan Costs." (Please see the appendix for a summary of different types of mutual fund average expense ratios.)

✦ **Manager Tenure**—There is a steady movement of talent within the investment-management world. As individuals move from firm to firm, the portfolios they are running don't shut down. The investment firm just brings on another manager. As you look back over the investment performance history, you want to ask yourself if the same manager is responsible for these returns. If it is someone new, what is her prior track record? Portfolio manager changes are less important for index funds and plain-vanilla bond funds than they are for actively managed stock funds.

✦ **Fund Size**—In the world of mutual funds, bigger is not necessarily better.[15] Some have gotten so big that their sheer size dilutes performance. When a fund has too much money to invest, it must buy larger stocks and/or invest in more securities. This causes funds, which may have once invested in small or mid-caps, to become large-cap funds. Further, the impact of individual successful stocks becomes diluted in a big portfolio. When a fund has tens of billions of assets, it is limited to investing in only the largest companies to soak up its cash. At this point it begins to resemble a high-cost index fund and begs the question: Why pay active management prices for a de facto index fund?

✦ **Top Ten Holdings and Portfolio Composition**—Mutual funds are required to disclose their holdings twice a year. Although the information is always dated, the portfolio composition can be instructive, especially if the turnover rate is low. I specifically look at the percentage of assets held in the top ten holdings as well as the total number of offerings. Depending on the client, a fund concentrated among thirty securities may not be as appropriate as one with a hundred holdings.

✦ **Turnover Ratio**—This refers to the fund's frequency of replacing its entire portfolio within a twelve-month period. A turnover ratio of 100 percent means that the entire portfolio turns over once a year. The issue for most investors is taxation of dividends and capital gains. The higher the turnover the more likely the chance of paying taxes. In a qualified plan, however, the issue is not taxation but rather trading costs. Every time a manager buys or sells a stock, there are costs that are charged back to the fund which ultimately reduces performance.

✦ **Style Consistency**—Different funds have different charters; some are more loosely defined than others. When it comes to retirement plans, style consistency or the notion of the fund's "truth in advertising" is a virtue. Offering funds that pursue specific investment objectives and stay within tightly defined investment parameters allows participants to create truly diversified portfolios with minimal overlap.

One of the advantages of working with mutual funds is the SEC-enforced requirement for disclosing material information on a regular basis. As a plan sponsor, you can research most mutual funds over the Internet. You can also subscribe to a mutual-fund database, such as Morningstar or Lipper to access this information. Or you can hire an investment consultant to perform the required investment analysis. (We will discuss the role of third-party advisers in chapter 13, "Putting It All Together—Vendor Selection.")

ONGOING MONITORING

At this point, you've looked at your company demographics and plan statistics. You've determined core asset classes, delineated your selection and monitoring criteria, selected funds, and recorded the process on paper in the IPS. The next step is to monitor the investments on a regular basis. This means tracking performance against the monitoring criteria on some regular basis such as semi-annually or annually. By tracking each fund's performance on a regular basis, you can ensure that each fund remains true to its purpose and meets the minimum benchmark requirements as set forth in the investment policy statement. Also, by keeping meeting notes, you demonstrate commitment to a due-diligent process. Over time, you may have to replace a fund that consistently fails to meet the minimum criteria for continued inclusion in the plan.

Investments are the backbone of a great 401(k) plan. That said, you may have the best investment lineup in the world but if no one participates in the plan, all your hard work is in vain. This brings us to employee education and communication, our next topic.

Notes

1. "Plan sponsors are sometimes under the mistaken impression that participant-directed 401(k) plans remove the fiduciary obligations traditionally found under defined benefit plans." "A Matter of Policy," Meg Glinksa, *CFO*, August 2000, p. 100.

   From a fiduciary perspective, ERISA does not distinguish between trustee and individually directed plans. As a fiduciary, you are either making investment choices for everyone in the plan (trustee-directed) or selecting the core investment lineup from which participants will create their own portfolios (participant-directed). Either way, you shoulder the responsibility of acting as the steward of other people's money.

2. "*Failure to prudently select*: When a plan fiduciary or committee fails to properly select the investment managers for the 401(k) plan, the participants might seek to recover the difference between what they actually earned and what they might have earned had an appropriate selection been made.
   Failure to monitor: In a participant-directed plan, if the plan fiduciaries fail to monitor the performance on a periodic basis and that performance over time is found to be deficient in comparison to benchmark indexes, the fiduciary might be charged to

make up the difference between actual performance and the benchmark index per-formance under the theory that the fiduciary failed to monitor the investments and to take corrective action."

The 401(k) Plan Management Handbook, Jeffrey M. Miller and Maureen M. Phillips, Irwin Professional Publishing, 1996, p. 145-146.

3. 7,181 stocks; 12,549 mutual funds—Morningstar Principia Pro—through March 31, 2001.

4. ERISA requires a plan fiduciary to "discharge his duties with respect to a Plan sole-ly in the interest of the participants and beneficiaries . . . by diversifying the invest-ments of the Plan so as to minimize the risk of large losses, unless under the circumstances it is clearly prudent not to do so." 29 U. S. C. §1104(a)(1)(C).

   No statute or regulation specifies what constitutes "diversifying" plan invest-ments, but the legislative history provides this guidance:

   > The degree of investment concentration that would violate this require-ment to diversify cannot be stated as a fixed percentage, because a fiduci-ary must consider the facts and circumstances of each case. The factors to be considered include (1) the purposes of the plan; (2) the amount of the plan assets; (3) financial and industrial conditions; (4) the type of invest-ment, whether mortgages, bonds or shares of stock or otherwise; (5) dis-tribution as to geographical location; (6) distribution as to industries; (7) the dates of maturity. H. R. Rep. No. 1280, 93 Cong., 2d Sess. (1974), reprinted in 1974 U. S. Code Cong. & Admin. News 5038, 5084-85 (Conference report at 304).

5. Although retail funds offer many advantages, they are not perfect. The most com-mon criticisms are listed below:

   + Some do not follow their investment mandate (style drift).
   + Some are expensive.
   + Very few actively managed funds consistently outperform their best-fit index.

✦ Some have problems with cash flows (i.e., having to keep a portion of the fund's assets in a cash reserve) since they are subject to the whims of after tax investors who may pull their money out at the slightest hint of trouble.

✦ Many are run solely to maximize the collection of assets with its heavy emphasis on marketing past performance and not necessarily to meet long-term goals and objective of investors in long-term retirement plans.

6. Putting money into actively managed mutual funds was often derided as a "loser's game" by the financial press during the last years of the great bull market, since many of the large, well-known funds underperformed the S&P 500 Index. At the same time, these popular "financial journalists" extolled the virtues of buying and selling individual securities. The end of the bull market has greatly reduced the number of "do-it-yourself" and "day trading" proponents.

7. Besides its stable of well-known no-load funds, Fidelity also offers another set of funds known as the "Advisor" series which they distribute through third-party intermediaries.

8. U.S. mutual fund companies spent $220 million to advertise their wares in print and on television in the first six months of this year, a 29 percent increase from the first half of 1996, according to Competitrack, a New York firm that tracks advertising.

9. Market capitalization is a convenient way to categorize stocks and is defined as the share price multiplied by the number of shares outstanding. Morningstar uses the five bands below to categorize the stocks and mutual funds it tracks in its databases.

✦ **Giant**—greater than $45,323 billion
✦ **Large**—between $8,711 and $45,323 billion
✦ **Mid**—between $1,388 and $8,711 billion
✦ **Small**—between $245 million and $1,388 billion
✦ **Micro**—less than $245 million

Morningstar Principia Pro, April 30, 2002.

10. In 2001, approximately 12% of 401(k) assets were invested in Index Funds. In 2001, approximately 12% of 401(k) assets were invested in Index Funds.

    Source: Speech made by a Consultant from Cerulli Associates, Inc. at the Scudder Investments Consultant Symposium held on February 1, 2002 in Key Biscayne, FL—Slide 14

    CA Research, BARRA RogersCasey

11. "The use of self-directed brokerage accounts has increased 75% over the last year, and is now offered in 14% of the plans surveyed." Morgan Stanley Dean Witter Investment Management 2000 Survey of the 401(k) Market.

12. "About 2,000 U.S. companies, covering 6 million of the nation's 40 million 401(k) participants, offer their own stock as an investment option in their employees' plans, said David Wray, president of the Profit Sharing/401(k) Council of America in Chicago, a non-profit trade group.", "Sad Chapter in Enron Saga: Case Underlines Danger of Stock as 401(k) Match", Liz Pulliam Weston and James T. Madore, *Chicago Tribune*, December 4, 2001.

    "As of October 31, 2001, nearly 30 percent of the assets held in 1.5 million plans were in the stock of the sponsoring company, the paper (New York Times) reported, citing management consultants Hewitt Associates LLC.", "Many 401(k) Plans Too Reliant on Companies Own Stock, NYT Says", Josh P. Hamilton, *Bloomberg News*, December 2, 2001.

13. Problems with company stock involve the following:

    + Valuation methodology
    + Liquidity and the costs associated with trading a thinly traded stock
    + Insider trading issues
    + Investment risk associated with investing in one security

    "Of the more than 2,400 employers surveyed in the last PLANSPONSOR DC Survey, 16% offered company stock as an investment option for their plan. An average of 55% of plans with greater than $200MM in total assets offered the option, while plans with fewer than $200MM averaged 12%. Despite advances in employee education and advice, 25% of participant balances remain in company stock across all plan sizes." 401(k) Pathfinder Mailing from PLANSPONSOR.com, May 2002.

14. "Plan sponsors are increasingly using investment consultants to guide them through the investment buying and monitoring process." Morgan Stanley Dean Witter Investment Management 2000 Survey of the 401(k) Market.

15. "Biggest Funds Aren't Always Best," Anne Willette, *USA Today,* June14, 1996.

CHAPTER 10

EMPLOYEE COMMUNICATION, EDUCATION, AND INVESTMENT ADVICE

Employee education is an essential part of any 401(k) plan. As average account balances grow, and as vendors offer more and more investment choices, the need for employee education increases.[1] In response, companies are beefing up their investment education efforts because employees are demanding the tools necessary to give them retirement answers. This trend is borne out by a recent survey in which employee-benefit professionals cited investment education as their top benefit priority.[2]

You can design the perfect 401(k)—top-notch investments, state-of-the-art recordkeeping, solid plan design, and low costs—but if employees don't participate, don't put enough money into the plan, or don't allocate their money in a way appropriate to their retirement time horizon, then the plan isn't working. This is where communication, education, and investment advice come into play.

EMPLOYEE EDUCATION VERSUS COMMUNICATION: DEFINITIONS

Some people use the terms "communication" and "education" interchangeably. I distinguish between the two primarily by their subject matter. Communication conveys core plan information, such as plan design features, operational and administrative procedures, and participants' rights under the law. Education is broader, as it seeks to communicate basic retirement and investment concepts. The distinction between the two is important, since many plan sponsors think that by communicating operational plan details they are educating, or vice versa. When you confuse the two, you run the risk of giving short shrift to one or the other.

Education and communication go hand in hand. You can't have one without the other, since both can have a profound impact on participants' behavior and a plan's ultimate success or failure. (We will be discussing what determines a successful plan later, in chapter 12, "A Good Plan.") The difference between the two is timing and emphasis. If a plan is properly communicated, most participants will understand basic plan operations or at least will know how to get the information they need when they need it. Employee education, on the other hand, is an ongoing effort that seeks to answer the fundamental questions, "What is my retirement goal?" and "What steps do I need to take to reach it?"

PLAN COMMUNICATIONS

Communicating basic information is often the easiest way to begin to address employee-education issues. This means making sure that eligible nonparticipants know, for example, how to enroll, how the loan provision works, and how their contributions affect their take-home pay. The last thing you want is someone not enrolling because he doesn't understand how the plan works. This should seem obvious, but the data suggests that many participants still do not understand the fundamentals. Consider the following findings from a survey conducted by the Association for the Advancement of Retired People (AARP).[3]

+ More than one in ten (13 percent) of those currently participating in employer-sponsored plans incorrectly believe that they never have to pay taxes on investments in the plan, while 6 percent mistakenly believe they have already paid taxes.

✦ Only 14 percent of workers with retirement plans know that 59½ is the age when they can withdraw money from 401(k) plans without penalty.

✦ Fully 30 percent of participants erroneously believe that monies withdrawn early from retirement plans are taxed at normal rates without penalties, and 4 percent believe that no taxes are ever paid on withdrawn funds.

✦ Nearly 20 percent of defined contribution plan participants do not know they can lose money in stocks and 65 percent do not know they could lose money in a bond fund.[4]

Understanding plan basics is essential to making informed decisions and avoiding misunderstandings. The key is to keep it simple. The Internet is especially well suited for communicating basic plan information since it allows participants to access information at a time and place of their own choosing.

EMPLOYEE EDUCATION

Ten years ago, handing out a Summary Plan Description (SPD) along with a packet of investment fact sheets was standard education fare. Today we know that that approach does not answer the questions heard most often from bewildered participants—"What should I do?" and "How should I invest my money?" Helping participants to answer these questions for themselves is at the heart of a solid employee-education program.

Finding answers to these broad, open-ended questions means zeroing in on the following specific questions:

✦ How much money will I need at retirement?

✦ Where am I now relative to my retirement goal?

✦ What steps must I take now to achieve my goals?

The purpose of a well-designed education campaign is to help employees answer these questions in a manner as cost- and operationally efficient as possible.

WHY BOTHER TO EDUCATE?

Before we look at specific communication and education (C&E) techniques, we need to examine the underlying assumption of this chapter: C&E is something an employer must do to insure the success of the plan. Some sponsors think that just offering the plan means they've done their job. If employees don't sign up, their line of reasoning goes, that's just too bad. As we'll see, this view is shortsighted. There are several reasons why plan sponsors want to educate their participants.

- ✦ It is a proven way to increase participation and average deferral percentages, which, in turn, has a positive impact on annual discrimination testing.
- ✦ It helps to fulfill ERISA 404(c) requirements and should reduce the likelihood of future participant litigation.
- ✦ It increases employee appreciation of the plan.
- ✦ It's the right thing to do. For most participants, education is the key to making informed financial decisions and the key to a comfortable retirement.

C&E—IT WORKS

If executed properly, a well-designed employee C&E campaign can have a dramatic effect on participation, average deferral percentages, and asset-allocation patterns, three essential elements of a successful plan. (We discuss the attributes of successful plans in chapter 12, "A Good Plan.") As we saw in chapter 4, "401(k) Compliance Tests," raising the participation and average deferral percentages will ensure that the plan passes its annual discrimination testing. And in chapter 6,

"Plan Design, Part II: Employer-Matching Contributions," we discussed the dramatic effect employer contributions can have on participation. Even for a company that does not spend much money on contributions, employee C&E can have a powerful impact on a plan's "vital statistics."

In an excellent 1996 study (see table, page 84), a national benefits consulting firm found that C&E can play as great a role in boosting savings and participation as the employer match rate.[5] This is good news for employers who either cannot afford or are reluctant to implement a generous matching formula. This survey and others like it[6] suggest that companies with a modest match but a strong C&E effort, can achieve the same rates of overall savings and participation as a company with a larger match but less effective communications.

Finally, employee C&E will do more than ensure good participation and raise contributions. It will also increase your employees' appreciation of the plan. Failure to provide C&E becomes a wasted opportunity for an employer to show off a valuable and highly appreciated employee benefit.

ERISA 404(c) AND EDUCATION

Besides being effective, compliance with ERISA 404(c) is another big reason companies are spending more time and money on employee education. As we saw in chapter 3, "Fiduciary Responsibility," in 1992 the Department of Labor (DOL) spelled out voluntary guidelines, which, if followed, would absolve the plan sponsor of his fiduciary liability for poor investment results in participant-directed plans. These rules are what are known as 404(c) regulations. In order to comply, a plan sponsor must meet the following minimum requirements:

+ The plan must offer participants a "broad range" of investment options.
+ The plan must allow for at least quarterly transfers between options, depending upon volatility.

✦ The plan must provide "sufficient information" to enable participants to make "informed decisions."[7]

Most plans meet the first and second conditions.[8] The last item, regarding "sufficient information," refers to employee-education requirements and the area to which we now turn.

DOL INTERPRETIVE BULLETIN 96-01

In 1996, the DOL responded to concerns about where to draw the line between investment "education" and investment "advice." The DOL clarified several formerly "gray" areas, explicitly citing them as specific examples of employee education.

✦ **Plan information**—information about the operation of the plan, benefits of participation and increasing contributions, etc.

✦ **General investment information**—material about general and financial investment concepts, historic rates of return of different asset classes, the effects of inflation, etc.

✦ **Asset-allocation models**—models of asset-allocation portfolios based on hypothetical individuals, etc.

✦ **Interactive investment materials**—materials that help participants quantify future retirement-income needs[9]

According to the DOL, examples of employee education include such concepts as compound growth, historical rates of return of various asset classes, and the relationship between risk and return. In contrast, telling a participant which funds to invest in would be considered advice. Most plan sponsors feel comfortable with the distinction and appear to be following 404(c) guidelines.[10]

✦   ✦   ✦

EMPLOYER OBLIGATION

Plan sponsors play a huge role in making employee retirement goals happen. A well-designed retirement plan is crucial and within that plan, the element of employee education is vitally important.

Americans are still woefully unprepared for retirement. The personal savings rate of the country has been steadily lagging behind the rest of the industrialized world for years.[11] Not surprisingly, "How much should I save?" and "How do I save?" are questions too many Americans still cannot answer. The key is education. As we have seen, participation rates and savings rates are indications of whether your plan is working or not. You may have a beautifully designed plan but if employees are not using it, if they are making poor investment choices, it's not working. Giving employees the necessary information they need to make informed decisions is crucial to the success of the plan and the financial security of the individual.[12]

WHAT EMPLOYEES WANT

When employees are asked what they want in terms of education and how they would like to receive this information, the answers are quite clear. Employees don't want to be bogged down with too much detail. Ideally, participants prefer the information to be presented verbally and, when appropriate, they prefer charts and graphs over text to illustrate key concepts.[13] The preferred approach is a one-on-one conversation with someone (87 percent). Although this may not be appropriate in all circumstances, people prefer to talk with an expert to help them navigate the retirement planning decision-making process. Other techniques favored by employees include financial planning/retirement planning seminars (81 percent), brochures and newsletters (79 percent), and videotapes on planning (73 percent).[14]

✦　✦　✦

Designing an Employee-Education Campaign

Well-designed and executed employee-education campaigns don't just happen. They require planning, an understanding of your current situation and an idea of future goals. Designing an employee-education campaign is similar to putting together an advertising campaign. You have to decide on three critical factors: message, media, and frequency. The best way to begin is to break the process down into simple steps by asking yourself the following questions:

+ **What are my goals?** Asking this question is a critical first step. Are you trying to address an easily measurable goal, like raising participation, increasing average deferral percentages, changing overall asset allocation, or slowing the rate of employee turnover? Or are the goals "soft" in nature, such as discussing different investment styles? In order to know if the campaign is a success, you first have to know where you are and where you want to go.

+ **Who is my target audience?** What kind of employees do you have: white collar, blue collar, pink collar, a combination? What is their level of investment knowledge? Is the workforce younger, older, mostly male, or mostly female? Do you have high turnover, low turnover? If you already have a plan, can your recordkeeper track demographics and pinpoint problem areas? For example, can you get current information about eligible nonparticipants, low savers, and people close to retirement? By segmenting the group and tailoring the message to a particular audience, you will significantly improve your chances of achieving the campaign's overall goals.[15]

+ **What message do I want to deliver?** Don't overestimate your group. Few people truly understand the cost of their retirement, what role Social Security will play in their future, and how important a 401(k) plan can be to their financial well-being.

Many people also don't understand basic investment concepts like tax-deferred compound growth, the importance of diversification in reducing risk, historical rates of return for various asset classes, and the insidious effect of inflation on future purchasing power. These concepts have never been adequately explained to them in a way that's relevant to their lives. The trick here is to chunk down basic retirement ideas and to focus on one or two at a time. If your group is older, information about distribution options and continued equity exposure throughout retirement will probably be important topics of interest. If the group is younger, information about the importance of saving from an early age, historical rates of return for different asset classes, and estimating the cost of retirement is appropriate.

✦ **What are the "best" media to reach my employees?** What's worked well in the past at your firm? What communication networks already exist at the company: Intranet, bulletin board, staff leaders, company newsletter? What media are best suited to carry the message and convey the information to your audience? Are all available media being used: "dummy statements" (a customized statement for a non-participating employee that quantifies the opportunity cost of their lack of participation), videotape, group and one-on-one meetings, Web-casting, payroll stuffers, Internet? There is no single "best" media, and a well-conducted campaign usually involves a combination of several types. People have different learning styles, education backgrounds, and attitudes about saving. In addition, company logistics (e.g., hourly/salary, union/nonunion, headquarters/branch, Internet access, etc.) will also play a role in the choice of media. For example, companies who have multistate, multisite locations or large numbers of employees working from remote locations will have different media requirements compared to companies with a single location.

That said, certain techniques consistently work to produce superior results.[16] First, one-on-one meetings with objective financial consultants are an effective tool. Also, customized paycheck comparisons that show employees how much a specific contribution will affect take-home pay and how much a person can expect at retirement, assuming different investment strategies can have a noticeable effect.[17] These statements can also be created for nonparticipants (i.e., "dummy" statements) to show them the opportunity cost of their nonparticipation over time. Targeted e-mails can also quickly raise participant awareness about plan changes or important events (e.g., open enrollment dates, etc.) Finally, easy-to-use interactive tools (usually Internet-based) allow participants to quickly determine how much retirement savings they'll need and what combination of savings rate and mix of asset classes will help them to achieve their goal.

✦ **Internal versus external help.** Do you have the time, resources, and expertise to conduct an education campaign internally? Does your plan and company culture require the customization of materials? If yes, can you produce the materials in-house or will you have to outsource this function? Or, like most companies, are you planning to piggyback off of the service provider's resources? (It makes sense to think of the service provider's Interactive Voice Response (IVR), call center, and Web site as the first line of employee education infrastructure.) Make sure you understand what your service provider can and cannot do. Many providers, for example, are not staffed to meet with participants on an individual basis. If you use a broker or a consultant, they should be able to help. If not, perhaps it makes sense to hire an outside firm to provide ad hoc employee education services. If you do hire an outside firm, make sure that they agree to well-defined goals that can be easily measured.

✦ **Determine budget and time constraints.** How much time and money can you afford? Are the goals and the media to be used consistent with your budget constraints?

✦   ✦   ✦

PUTTING IT ALL TOGETHER

After you decide on the goals, the audience, the message, the media, and the overall budget constraints (time and money), the next step is to implement the campaign. The following tips will go a long way toward maximizing your chances of success.

+ **Take Care of Legal Requirements—SPD and Prospectus:** Be certain that the Summary Plan Description is in order and that all participants receive a copy at least once a year or can access a copy from a shared location. If you are using mutual funds, make sure that participants receive prospectus information. Both documents are legally required. A plan "detail" or plan "highlight" sheet that provides a simple overview of the plan (e.g., eligibility, company match, investment options) is also recommended.

+ **Measure Results:** The key to any successful campaign is the ability to measure its impact over time. Thus, knowing where you stand allows you to establish a baseline and gives you a starting point from which to measure how successful your campaign is. We will discuss benchmarking your plan and surveying participants in more detail in chapter 12, "A Good Plan (Benchmarking)."

+ **Repeat Periodically:** Employee education is an ongoing effort. It's likely that you will need to repeat a campaign over time in order to reinforce the message. Also, as your company's workforce changes over time, you may have to design a new campaign that is more suited to the changing realities.

INVESTMENT ADVICE

Despite the important role education plays in positively affecting participants' behavior, there is a group of employees for whom education is still not enough.[18] When all is said and done, these employees just want someone to tell them exactly what to do and where to invest. This is where advice comes into play. Advice is a growing trend and the topic to which we now turn.

According to the Investment Advisers Act of 1940, an investment advisor is someone who is compensated for providing investment advice. Depending on the scope of their business, advisors must be registered with either the state in which they do business or the Securities Exchange Commission (SEC). All of the major 401(k) service providers have allied themselves with at least one of the national advice providers and make the Internet-based service available for their plan-sponsor clients.[19] These advice firms provide high quality, low-cost investment advice delivered primarily over the Internet. Their personalized services, based on detailed retirement questionnaires and personal information, tells participants which specific 401(k) investment options to select and in what percentages. The advice market is booming and will continue to grow.[20] Not only does the demand for advice increase with the rise in average account balances, but the Department of Labor and pending legislation has sanctioned investment managers to provide advice for their own investments.[21] Advice is clearly the next "new" thing in the defined-contribution marketplace.

It used to be that many sponsors did not offer advice for fear of increased fiduciary liability, but employer attitudes are rapidly changing. The DOL has gone to great lengths to assuage sponsor concerns and to encourage them to offer advice to participants. They have spoken clearly on several important issues surrounding this topic:[22]

+ Many workers need investment advice.
+ Employers are not liable for acts of investment advisors.
+ Prudent selection of an investment advisor limits the employer's liability.

In a recent *Newsweek* article, Jane Bryant Quinn, one of the country's most popular personal-finance experts, concluded that all good companies will ultimately engage the services of an investment advisory firm on behalf of their employees.[23]

The Enron 401(k) scandal illustrates the need of many plan participants to seek independent, third-party objective advice, since the consequences of poor decision-making can be catastrophic. When a company hires an independent advisory firm, the firm becomes a fiduciary to the plan and would be named in the case of a participant-driven lawsuit. As a fiduciary, you are still responsible for the decision to hire the advisor but that risk is no greater than for any other fiduciary decision.[24] This means that you should use the same procedural due diligence that you would use in hiring any service provider, a topic we will discuss in detail in chapter 13, "Putting It All Together—Vendor Selection."

In summary, participant-education and communication work. The key is creating a focused campaign based on clearly defined goals and targeted to the right audience. Customized information is a powerful technique for influencing participant behavior. However, despite your best efforts at education, there is still a segment of the population for whom investment advice is necessary in answering the fundamental question about how to invest their money. Taken together, communication, education, and advice can have a powerful impact on the overall success of your plan.

Your ability to keep plan costs down also has a direct bearing on retirement balances and the ultimate success of the plan. We will discuss plan costs now.

Notes

1. Most plans (86 percent) say they provide investment education to employees. This is a significant increase from the 1997 survey, in which 59 percent said they provided investment education. Six out of ten plans that provide investment education indicate they maintain an ongoing communication campaign aimed at informing employees on 401(k) plan investing matters. "Trends & Experience in 401(k) Plans," Hewitt Associates, 1999.

2. "Survey of Certified Employee Benefit Specialists Top Five Benefit Priorities for

1998," conducted by International Society of Certified Employee Benefit Specialists and Deloitte & Touche LLP.

Top five employee priorities for 2001, according to the ISCEBS/Deloitte & Touche Survey:

- Reducing health care costs
- Evaluating, implementing, and expanding the use of Internet and Intranet applications (57.9 percent)
- Expanding the use of employee self-service technology for communications and administration (45.4 percent)
- Providing financial and retirement planning tools and information (42.8 percent)
- Providing increased investment education (35.7 percent)

3. "Working Americans Contributing to 401(k) and Other Qualified Retirement Plans Remain in Dark on Important Details," *Business Wire,* December 15, 1997.

4. "The Empowerment Myth", Elayne Robertson Demby, *PlanSponsor*, July 2001, p. 67. (Data comes from a 2001 survey of defined contribution plan participants conducted by Mathew Greenwald Associates.)

5. "The Word Can Be Mightier Than the Match," Watson Wyatt Worldwide, 1996.

6. "When seminars were instituted there was a 12.14 percentage point increase in partic-ipation among lower-paid employees. . . . Participation increased among highly com-pensated employees by 6.6 percentage points, for an overall increase of 7.65%." "The Business Case for Financial Education," *Pension Benefits*, v. 6, no. 8, August 1997.

"Forty-nine percent of respondents to Buck's annual '401(k) Plans: Employer Practices & Policies' survey, reported an increase in participation since implement-ing a savings education program." "How to Educate Your 401(k) Plan Participants," *Defined Contribution News*, 1997, p. 1.

"According to the 1996 update of *The Merrill Lynch Baby Boom Retirement Index*, . . . the typical retirement education program conducted in the work place raises the average rate of overall savings by 2.2%." The Eighth Annual Merrill Lynch Retirement and Financial Planning Survey of Employers, 1996, p.18.

7. It should be noted that even though a plan may fulfill 404(c) requirements, it is not absolved of selecting good investment options and monitoring their performance. See chapter 9, "Investments."

8. As we will see later in chapter 12, the vast majority of plans are valued daily, and the average number of funds offered is twelve.

9. "Investment Education Guidance Includes Safe Harbors," *Employee Benefit Plan Review,* March 1996, p. 17.

10. "Virtually all 401(k) plans that offer participant choice follow the mandates of 404c which recommends a minimum number of investment choices and describes the types of information that should be provided to employees about their 401(k) investments." "401(k) Is Nice, But Who Is Qualified?," Macgregor Hall, The Business Journal of Portland, December 28, 2001
    http://portland.bizjournals.com/portland/stories/2001/12/31/focus2.html

11. Why Do Americans Not Save More? Or Do They?
    http://www.ncpa.org/pd/economy/pd102999f.html
        The savings rate, or the pro-portion of personal disposable income that goes into savings, in the United States is far lower than that for the rest of the industrialized world. For Japan, the savings rate is almost 20 percent; Germany, nearly 15 percent; Canada, France, and Italy, well over 5 percent. The U.S. savings rate? In 1994, it was just 3.1 percent.
    http://www.multimedia.calpoly.edu/development/busen/alpha/s/savings.html

    List of savings rates from 1959 to 2002
    http://www.stls.frb.org/fred/data/gdp/psavert

12. "Even before Enron became a household word, it was an open secret in the pension world that too many people were making lousy investment decisions with their 401(k) money. If they weren't overdosing on company stock, they were being too cautious, not diversifying enough or diversifying irrationally." "First Came 401(k)'s. Now, Some Advice", Fran Hawthorne, *New York Times*, March 12, 2002.

13. "Qualitative Analysis: Evaluation of Employer Sponsored Savings Program Enrollment Information," Prepared by Elrick & Lavidge for American Century, September 1996.

14. Chart 23, "Perceived Effectiveness of Investment Education Materials or Assistance and Percentage Citing Effectiveness of Each," The Seventh Annual Merrill Lynch Retirement and Financial Planning Survey of Employers, 1996, p.17.

15. "Plan sponsors are increasingly looking to service providers to segment their employee populations and create targeted communication efforts to address their needs. Of the survey population, this is the most cited method (49% of the time) to communicate with plan participants in the coming year." "Morgan Stanley Dean Witter Investment Management 2000 Survey of the 401(k) Market."

16. "How to Educate Your 401(k) Plan Participants: Issues, Principles, Best Practices," *Defined Contribution News*, 1997, p. 19. "Effectiveness of Communication Techniques," Source: Profit Sharing/401(k) Council of America. January 1995 survey of 261 profit sharing and 401(k) plans.

17. According to research from Watson Wayatt, a national benefits consulting firm, "employees who receive personalized statements contribute .85% more of their salary to the 401(k) plan on average, compared to employees who don't receive this information." "How to Increase Employee Participation," *http://www. 401kHelpCenter.com*, February 20, 2002.

18. "While the role of the 401(k) is firmly established, a number of studies suggest that many plan participants have been unwittingly thrust into a role for which they are ill-prepared. Aside from mistakes in saving strategies such as failing to participate early in a plan or failing to maximize contributions, many plan participants are likely to be making investment choices that are not ideal for their goals, objectives, and effective investment horizons. Due to perceived cost and factors, almost 80% of Americans do not receive any professional financial advice." *401k Checkup: Best Practices in the Measurement and Disclosure of Risk in 401(k) Plans*, RiskMetrics Group, Inc. February 2002.

19. The major Internet-based advice providers are Financial Engines, Mpower, and Morningstar.

20. Over the last year, the provision of online investment advice services to participants in employer-sponsored retirement plans has begun to come into its own. Spurred on by encouragement from the Department of Labor, the number of employers implementing online investment advice services has increased, as have partnerships between advice service vendors and plan providers.
Online Investment Advice Services Becoming More Common Workplace Financial Planning Offering
By Sue Burzawa
http://www.spencernet.com/Archive/EBPRarticles4.html#Anchor-23269

21. Historically, the law prohibited investment managers from giving investment advice in order to prevent conflict of interest (e.g., the investment manager would recommend his own investments), but this is changing. The DOL's Advisory Opinion 2001–09 removes some of the economic barriers that have historically kept investment managers from offering the service. The opinion says that "an investment management firm could be compensated for offering investment advice on its own funds and could receive higher fees based on participant investment decisions on that advice subject to certain conditions."

22. "U.S. Department of Labor's Leslie Kramerich Talks About Investment Advice Before Pension Actuaries," PWBA Press Release, September 15, 2000.
www.dol.gov/dol/pwba/public/media/press/pr091500.htm

23. March 4, 2002 - Newsweek
Help! I'm Scared for My 401(k)
Jane Bryant Quinn
Reported by Temma Ehrenfeld
At the end of the day, what would really help employees manage their 401(k)s? Good investment advice, that's what. Your company may distribute an educational booklet that shows pretty pie charts and defines words like "diversification." But after all the reading is done—after you decide whether you're a conservative, mod-

erate or aggressive investor—two questions remain: How should you invest your money and should you own company stock?

http://204.29.171.80/framer/navigation.asp?realname=Newsweek&charset=utf-8&cc=US&lc=en-US&uid=356645&frameid=1&providerid=113&url=http%3A%2F%2Fwww.newsweek.com

24. "In the mid-90's, the Labor Department expanded its guidelines to encourage employers to give more advice, as long as it comes from an independent adviser and not directly from the employer or the investment company that manages the assets. These rulings were meant to alert employers that there was no "untoward fiduciary liability" if the employer chose the adviser prudently and monitored the service, says Olena Berg Lacy, the assistant Labor Secretary in charge of pensions during the Clinton administration.," "First Came 401(k)'s. Now, Some Advice," Fran Hawthorne, *New York Times*, March 12, 2002.

CHAPTER 11

PLAN COSTS

Nowhere is there more confusion about 401(k) plans than in the area of costs and fees. Unfortunately, ignorance about this subject can be dangerous to your participants' (and your) retirement. Since participants pay for most of the costs in the form of asset-based fees,[1] they are heavily penalized when an employer chooses a "high cost" plan. The majority of the costs come straight out of participants' investment returns and can seriously erode retirement balances. Sponsor ignorance coupled with lack of adequate vendor disclosure continues to contribute to this serious problem.

This chapter is designed to provide a quick yet thorough overview of this important topic so that you can make an informed buying decision. The chapter will describe the importance of fees, illustrate the different ways vendors charge fees, show you how to quickly analyze a service provider's cost structure, define "high," "low," and "moderate" plan costs, and, finally, offer rules of thumb proven to keep plan costs low.

THE IMPORTANCE OF UNDERSTANDING PLAN COSTS

When average account balances were small, sponsors could more easily ignore the issue of plan costs. That's no longer the case today as account balances have mushroomed, and participants pay for the majority of a plan's costs in the form of asset-based fees. Sadly, sponsor understanding of this important issue has not kept pace with the growth of account balances, especially in the small-plan marketplace.[2] And many participants don't even know that they are paying fees at all.

What kind of impact are we talking about? Suppose you have thirty-five years until retirement, and a current 401(k) account balance of $25,000. Let's assume your average return is 7 percent, you don't contribute another dime to the account, and the annual fees are 0.5 percent. In thirty-five years, your account balance should grow to $227,000. If the fees were just one percentage point higher—1.5 percent—your account balance would be $163,000 at the end of thirty-five years. That's $64,000, or a 28 percent difference.[3]

There are a number of reasons for lack of sponsor understanding. First, when account balances were small, high fees had little impact because the effects were negligible. Second, they never directly affect the company's bottom line since participants bear the majority of plan costs anyway. Third, during the great bull market of the 1990s, there was little concern over fees when investments were routinely returning 20 percent a year. Finally, the way in which service providers price and package their products, especially at the small end of the marketplace, can be confusing to the uninformed buyer. Few vendors go out of their way to talk about how they price, and for some of the high-cost providers, it is in their best interest to remain quiet. If plan sponsors truly understood their responsibility to keep plan costs in check, and if participants understood the impact of excessive fees over time, there would be much more of an outcry.[4]

THE DOL STEPS IN

In chapter 3, we saw that one of the main duties of a fiduciary is to ensure that the fees paid to service providers are "reasonable." This is more than an academic exercise. As 401(k) plans play an expanding role in the U.S. retirement landscape, the careful design, operation, and administration of these plans has become a public policy issue and has caught the eye of the federal government. Olena Berg-Lacy, in her role as former Assistant Secretary of the U.S. Department of Labor, left no doubt about the DOL's stance when she said, "We want to make sure that plan sponsors pay attention to fee issues"[5] and "It is an employer's fiduciary duty to make sure the fees 401(k) participants pay are reasonable."[6] In an effort to clarify the situation and to give plan sponsors comparative cost information, the DOL held hearings on the issue of plan fees and costs in November 1997 and prepared a booklet the following year dedicated exclusively to the topic of 401(k) pricing[7]—the clearest sign yet of the topic's importance.

PARTICIPANTS AS ACTIVISTS

Increasingly, it is activist plan-participants that are leading the charge for lower costs. Spurred on by articles from popular financial magazines with headlines like "How to Protect Yourself Against the Great Retirement Rip-off"[8] or "How Funds Get Rich at Your Expense,"[9] participants are beginning to ask questions and demand answers. Don't be surprised if someone walks into your office and insists on knowing why the plan you selected costs so much. This is even more likely in the current bear-market environment as participants are increasingly focused on costs. As a buyer, you want to know what you're paying, what you're getting, and how it stacks up with the competition, so you can get the best deal and protect yourself against possible litigation.[10] And once you know, you'll want to fully disclose all fees to participants on a regular basis.

UNDERSTANDING PLAN COSTS

Determining the reasonableness of fees requires three separate steps. First, you have to know what the total costs are. Second, you have to compare these costs against some objective benchmark. And finally, you have to judge whether the costs you are paying are reasonable in light of the services received. The remainder of this chapter is devoted to giving you the tools necessary to understand any vendor's pricing formulas so you can make an informed buying decision.

VENDOR PRICING

In order to understand the fees and charges you and your participants pay, you have to first understand how vendors price their services. As a general rule, total plan assets and, in particular, average account balances, drive vendor pricing. The more money there is in a plan, and the higher the account balances, the lower the administrative fees and the greater the opportunity of using nonproprietary and lower-priced "institutional" investments. Other variables that affect vendor pricing include annual net cash flow, the number of company locations and payrolls, plan design complexity, potential merger and acquisition activity, and strategic fit.[11]

The next step is to determine whether the sponsor or the participant pays for each fee. Participants almost always pay the asset-based fees as they are netted out of the investment returns, and there is a growing trend toward shifting even the administrative fees to the participants as well. Finally, your plan fees have to be put into some kind of overall context of "high," "average," or "low." For example, a $1 million plan that pays 1.75 percent of plan assets in total fees (i.e., $17,500), may be "average," whereas for a $25 million plan, 1.75 percent would be considered "high" (i.e., $375,000). Determining the total cost of a plan is a relatively simple affair once you understand the types of fees and where they are hidden. (See the appendix for a useful chart to help in breaking down plan costs.)

BILLED (EXPLICIT) EXPENSES

There are two sources of revenue for 401(k) service providers: explicit and implicit charges. Let's start with the easier of the two—explicit fees. Explicit fees are charges that are billed directly either to the plan sponsor or to plan participants. These charges are easy to determine since they should be clearly stated in your service provider's administrative services agreement. Below, I've listed some of the more common explicit fees:

+ One-time start up and conversion costs
+ Annual administrative, recordkeeping, and compliance-testing charges
+ Transaction-based charges like loans, hardships, and benefit distributions
+ Per diem fees for employee-education meetings
+ One-time termination charges
+ Investment transfer fees

Many service providers have gone out of their way to reduce or even eliminate explicit fees as a way to advertise "low-cost" or "no-cost" 401(k) plans. Recordkeeping fees often serve as a "loss leader" with the service providers hoping to make it up in more-lucrative asset-based fees. Whenever possible, the company should pay for these fees since these costs are tax deductible as a business expense. When participants pay, dollars are diverted from tax-advantaged investment growth, which represents a lost opportunity for dividends, interest, and gains. Unfortunately, more and more companies are shifting the burden of the explicit fees to participants.[12]

ASSET-BASED (IMPLICIT) FEES

Most service providers derive the majority of their revenue from asset-based fees. Unlike explicit fees, which are usually flat dollar charges, asset-based revenues are derived as a function of the plan assets. That's why, generally speaking, the more money inside your plan and the higher your plan's average account balance, the more attractive it is to the marketplace. Asset-based fees now account for nearly 90 percent of the revenue generated by 401(k) service providers.[13] As assets increase, that percentage will continue to grow, making the sponsor's understanding of these fees absolutely necessary. As we saw earlier, a relatively small fee of say, 0.5 to 1.5 percent over a period of time, can seriously erode a participant's retirement-account balance.

The implicit costs, or the costs associated with the investments, come in several different forms:

- ✦ Front-end and back-end loads
- ✦ Investment management fees
- ✦ 12b-1 and Sub Transfer Agent fees
- ✦ Asset-based "wrap" fees
- ✦ Spreads, market-value adjustments, and contract-termination fees

LOAD FUNDS

Front- or back-end loads, transaction costs charged when a participant buys shares of a fund either going into the plan (front-end) or exiting a fund (back-end), can be found in broker-dealer 401(k) products with less than $1 million of total assets. Although not a true asset-based fee per se, these charges occur every time a participant buys or sells a fund in which the loads pay for the broker's fees. When plan assets reach a certain critical mass, usually $1 million, the broker-dealer products generally purchase shares at Net Asset Value (NAV) with the front-end load waived.

TOTAL EXPENSE RATIO

Fund companies derive significant revenue from the internal operating expenses of their funds, and it should come as no surprise that many of the leading 401(k) service providers are also top investment firms. The cost of administering and recordkeeping tens of thousands of participants is the price they pay to efficiently gather assets. If you recall from chapter 1, gathering and managing assets is an extremely lucrative business and the 401(k) marketplace represents a way in which service providers can gain hundreds and thousands of individual shareholders overnight along with tens of millions of assets. And because of the long-term horizon of the average retirement investor, the money tends to stay put and continue to roll in despite the swings in the marketplace.

The expense ratio is the percentage of plan assets paid for fund operation, distribution, and management fees. Fund expenses are reflected in the daily share price, the Net Asset Value (NAV), after all of the expenses have been netted out of the returns. To a buyer, the total expense ratio, or the sum of all the individual components (e.g., investment management fee, custodial fee, 12b-1 fee if applicable, etc.), is far more important than the detail of the individual components. What the specific pieces tell us, however, is the story of how the funds are marketed.

12B-1 AND SUB-TRANSFER AGENCY (SUBTA) FEES

The second way vendors make money is by distributing other companies' products (funds). In chapter 7, we looked at the growth of fund "supermarkets" and "alliances" as the paradigm of choice for many 401(k) service providers. In brief, if an investment company is not large enough to distribute its own products, it must find others to distribute for them.[14] In a manner similar to how a grocery store operates,[15] service providers with "alliance" platforms collect revenue from the company whose funds they distribute in addition to the revenue their own investments generate. The distributors typically earn between 25 to 50 basis points, or $.25 to $.50 for every $100 of assets they sell, depending on the fund. And the most common way in which distributors get paid is through 12b-1 fees.[16] This common industry practice is known as "revenue sharing."

12b-1 Fees

Many funds have 12b-1 fees built into them as part of their operating expense. 12b-1 fees are used to pay for marketing and distribution costs and usually range from .25 to 1 percent, or 25 to 100 basis points.[17] A 401(k) service provider can usually expect to receive between .25 and .50 percent from the funds they distribute. That may not seem like a lot of money—.35 percent means you earn $3,500 for every million of assets—but with nearly $2 trillion of 401(k) money sloshing around, and nearly $6 trillion of assets held in mutual funds, the old saying remains true—a small percentage of a lot of money is a lot of money.

Sub-TA Fees

When you're putting together a typical investment alliance platform, revenue sharing is one of the main reasons (along with brand-name recognition, performance, cost, and manager tenure) for inclusion. Reimbursement for distribution usually comes in the form of 12b-1 fees but they may also include what are known as Sub-Transfer Agent (Sub TA) fees. These are fees between the service provider and the investment firm "that specify a payment from the investment management firm to the service provider in exchange for specified services."[18] Both the 12b-1 and Sub TA fees are spelled out in each fund's prospectus. At the close of each market day, the Net Asset Value (NAV) is calculated after netting out all of the internal operating expenses of the fund including the 12b-1 and Sub TA fees. Let's look in more detail at how an alliance works.

EXAMPLE: FIDELITY ADVISOR, FIDELITY DIRECT, AND VANGUARD FUNDS

Many alliance products will go out of their way to claim they offer Fidelity funds as part of their investment lineup. Upon closer inspection, however, most of these Fidelity funds are part of Fidelity's "Advisor" series. Fidelity has several kinds of funds grouped primarily by their distribution channel (e.g., "direct," "third-party," "institutional," etc.) Fidelity's "Advisor Funds," for example, are distributed by intermediaries, e.g., stockbrokers or commission-based financial planners, as well as third-party institutions such as banks and insurance companies.

Because of the need to pay for distribution, these funds have built into them 12b-1 fees between 50 and 75 basis points. The service provider usually collects 50 basis points for distributing one of these Fidelity funds. In addition, the vendor who offers Fidelity Funds can gain a marketing advantage by piggybacking off of Fidelity's well-known brand name.

In contrast, let's consider the Vanguard family of funds. Vanguard markets the majority of its funds directly to the public on a no-load basis.[19] The company aggressively markets itself as the industry's low-cost provider shunning both loads and 12b-1 fees. With no 12b-1s built into their funds, they lack the mechanism with which to compensate fund supermarkets and alliances for distribution. The upshot: despite Vanguard's low-cost expense structure and solid investment record, you usually won't find service providers distributing their funds. The explanation for this is just plain economics. Why would a service provider distribute Vanguard funds for free when they could distribute another company's comparable high-quality fund and get paid? If you do run across a Vanguard fund in the small plan marketplace, there is usually an additional asset-based fee layered over the fund's internal operating known as a "wrap" fee—which we will discuss next.

Asset-Based "Wrap" Fees

"Wrap" fees are common expense-recovery mechanisms in the start-up and small-plan marketplace (roughly defined as under $10 million of total assets) and are usually associated with insurance companies. With this type of fee, the insurance company establishes separate investment accounts using retail mutual funds as the underlying investment vehicle. The separate account then "wraps" an additional fee over and above the cost of the underlying investment. For example, if the fund's expense ratio were normally 1.25 percent, then the insurance company's asset-based wrap fee of 1 percent would raise the total cost of the investment to 2.25 percent.

The primary justification of a wrap fee is to (1) offset the upfront costs incurred in setting up a plan with little or no assets, and (2) pay a third-party broker or agent a commission for distributing the product and servicing the client. Wrap fees vary by vendor but they are usually based on the following criteria: total plan assets, explicit billed expenses, the amount and type of broker commissions, and the existence of a contract-termination charge. The amount of the wrap fee is determined by the amount of total plan assets. It should come as no surprise then that start-ups and small-plans with the least amount of assets have the highest wrap fees. As the plans grow in size, the wrap fee usually declines and, depending on the vendor, may even expire. During the course of the wrap fee's life however, the wrap fee lowers participants' net returns.

Insurance companies who use wrap fees denominate their investment's daily price in unit values as opposed to Net Asset Values (NAV) common to the mutual fund world. Although the two numbers track together (if the NAV of the underlying mutual fund goes up, the insurance company's unit value will also go up), they are not the same. This means that participants in wrap-fee programs cannot track their investments in the local paper since newspapers only show NAV data and not unit values.

OTHER CHARGES: "SPREADS," MARKET-VALUE ADJUSTMENTS, AND CONTRACT-TERMINATION CHARGES

Vendors have other, more subtle ways in which to earn revenue, and we briefly review them here. If you already have a plan, be sure to check your contract to see if any of these charges apply. If you haven't yet set up a plan, ask the prospective vendors if these charges pertain to your situation.

Some vendors require that the buyer use one of their "guaranteed" or stable value accounts. These accounts are like a CD paying a guaranteed rate of interest. The vendors make money on the spread between the interest rate they earn in the marketplace and the interest rate they pay. For example, if the insurance company earns 6.5 percent investing the assets, it credits only 5.5 percent to the investor, earning a spread of 1 percent, or 100 basis points.

When the GIC contract terminates, there is a reconciliation, or a market-value adjustment (MVA), between the contract's "book" and "market" values.[20] Depending on interest rates at the time of contract termination, there can be either a gain or loss. The MVA is the price paid for a stable-value contract where the principal is insured and there is no fluctuation in the price. In addition to the pure market-value adjustment, there may be an additional expense factor, depending on the contract.

Finally, some group annuity contracts will charge a "surrender fee" or "contract termination charge" if the plan terminates its contract within a specified period of time. This surrender charge is usually determined as a percentage of total assets and eventually expires. For example, a vendor may charge 7 percent if the contract terminates in year 1, 6 percent in year 2, 5 percent in year 3, and so on, until it expires in year 7.

WHERE TO FIND THE INFORMATION

Mutual funds are by definition "registered," meaning that they must disclose investment fees in a prospectus and are governed by the Securities Exchange Commission (SEC). Third-party investment databases—such as Morningstar, and Lipper—conveniently compile the investment information generally found in a prospectus. (Please see the appendix for a summary of average mutual fund expense ratios.) Banks and insurance company service providers, in addition to mutual funds, may also use nonregistered products such as collective trusts and group variable annuity products, which are not required to issue a prospectus. However, most vendors will gladly disclose their pricing formulas. It's up to you, the plan sponsor, to ask for a full explanation of all the fees and costs.

At this point, we are noting the various ways in which service providers charge fees in order to make money. The purpose is to help you understand pricing schemes. There is no right or wrong way. In the end, the cost of the plan has to be measured against what you can get in the marketplace for a plan your size, and the value the service providers bring to your plan.

"HIGH," "AVERAGE," AND "LOW" COSTS

Once you've determined what your costs are, the next step is to place the costs into some kind of context of "high," "average," or "low." Since asset-based fees account for 90 percent of total plan costs, it makes sense to first calculate the average expense ratio of your fund lineup and compare it to industry averages. [21] Be sure to add any asset-based wrap fee to the average portfolio cost if you use a product that imposes one. (See the appendix for a detailed breakout of average investment costs by fund style and market capitalization.)

The next step is to compare your total plan costs against national normative data. The table below lists some essential plan cost information taken from the "401(k) Averages Book."

	25 participants; $1,000,000 in assets	50 participants; $2,000,000 in assets	100 participants; $4,000,000 in assets	200 participants; $8,000,000 in assets
Average plan cost per participant	$637.60	$583.14	$560.59	$525.63
Average plan cost as a percentage of assets	Investment: 1.30% Record-keeping/ Administration: .24% Trustee: .05% Total Bundled: 1.59%	Investment: 1.26% Record-keeping/ Administration: .17% Trustee: .03% Total Bundled: 1.46%	Investment: 1.26% Record-keeping/ Administration: .13% Trustee: .01% Total Bundled: 1.40%	Investment: 1.20% Record-keeping/ Administration: .10% Trustee: .01% Total Bundled: 1.31%
Range of total plan costs	Low: $10,151 Average: $15,757 High: $23,781	Low: $16,900 Average: $29,053 High: $46,461	Low: $30,061 Average: $55,796 High: $90,621	Low: $47,330 Average: $104,772 High: $178,940

As you can see from the data, smaller plans usually pay more than larger plans, all things being equal. Also, fees can vary widely even among plans of similar asset sizes.

As a plan sponsor and fiduciary, fees are an important issue but there are two caveats to keep in mind. First, fees must be considered in the context of the scope and quality of the services received. Second, since most of the fees are netted out of the investment returns, total plan costs generally and investment fees in particular, can only be properly understood within a larger context of risk-adjusted investment returns. To focus solely on plan costs without considering the investment piece of the equation is to perform analysis that is too simple by half.

PRICING RULES OF THUMB

Although each vendor has its own pricing model, generally they use total liquid assets, average participant-account balances, net annual cash flow, and ratio of proprietary to nonproprietary investments in order to determine what, if any, explicit fees to charge. After looking at hundreds of plans of all different asset sizes, one can make certain generalizations about pricing.

+ Plan costs become a major issue as 401(k) assets and average account-balances increase. Plan sponsors can no longer afford to be uneducated about costs, as it is clearly their fiduciary duty to understand and control them.

+ The best way to look at total plan costs (explicit plus implicit fees) is as a percentage of plan assets over time. To look only at explicit costs is to miss where the majority of fees are found.

+ Explicit fees are tax deductible as a company business expense, while asset-based fees are not. If possible, it makes more sense to use tax-deductible dollars to pay for plan expenses than to use plan assets to pay for them. Dollars that are diverted from a tax-advantaged retirement account represent a lost opportunity for dividends, interest, and investment gains.

✦ The larger your plan's asset base and average account balance, the greater your ability to lower or negotiate away costs like start up, conversion fees, employee education, and annual record-keeping fees. More money also gives you a greater chance of reducing or eliminating asset-based "wrap" fees, adding "out-side" funds to your lineup, and, if your provider offers them, access to lower-cost "institutional" shares.

✦ Be careful of simplistic generalizations and absolute statements about pricing. Is a plan that costs 1 percent of total plan assets better than a plan that costs 1.25 percent? Is a fund with a 50 basis point 12b-1 fee and an expense ratio of 110 basis points worse than a similarly-priced fund with no 12b-1 fee? Absolutely not. Asset-based fees are a function of the underlying invest-ments, and the investments, in turn, must be evaluated in the con-text of risk-adjusted returns and relative peer group performance. In short, fees can only be understood within the context of a total value equation.

✦ Generally speaking, NAV pricing is less expensive than "wrap" fee pricing. However, this doesn't necessarily mean that you should always select a NAV product. A lot depends on fund selec-tion, investment performance, and the overall number and qual-ity of services provided. A plan may be better served with a modest wrap-fee product where employees are being actively counseled to join the plan, increase their savings percentage, and allocate their investments more appropriately. Also, what you gain in cost savings you may lose in fund selection, since the NAV provider may require your plan to use only their proprietary investments.

✦ Start up and small plans have the highest fees as measured by per-centage of assets. This should not be surprising, since many providers use wrap fees to offset the up-front costs incurred in setting up a start-up plan and to pay a third-party broker or agent a commission for distributing the product and servicing the client.

✦ Plan decision-makers can have a significant impact on the cost of the plan. You can lower the plan's overall expense structure by shopping around, being an informed buyer, and favoring high-quality, lower-cost investment vehicles. Over time, this could mean tremendous savings to the plan participants.

✦ Some vendors are consistently more expensive than others. There is variance not only between different kinds of vendors (insurance and mutual fund companies, for example) but also within categories. Some insurance and mutual fund companies are consistently more expensive (or less expensive) than their peers.

✦ If your plan is large enough, you may be able to qualify for lower-cost institutional fund pricing.[22] If you run a large plan (i.e., $250 million or more), you may consider collective trust funds, or even setting up your own proprietary funds.

✦ Voluntary full disclosure of all fees to participants should be your mantra. Not only do they have a right to know, but they will be demanding this information from you anyway.

Cost is an important consideration, yet it is not the only criteria in designing a plan. Breadth and quality of service, as well as overall investment performance, are also important considerations. The trick is to look at costs relative to services and to benchmark these against other comparable plans. We will discuss how to factor these various pieces into a buying equation in chapter 12, "A Good Plan (Benchmarking)" and chapter 13, "Putting It All Together—Vendor Selection."

✦   ✦   ✦

Notes

1. PSCA Annual Survey.

   According to Spectrem Group's projections, the aggregate 401(k) marketplace generates $13.204 billion of total fees, of which 89.5 percent ($11.817 billion) is derived from asset fees, while the remaining 10.5 percent ($1.387 billion) comes from service fees. "Plan Sponsors Need Better Fix on 401(k) Fees," *Employee Benefit Plan Review,* September 2001, p. 22.

2. "Seventy-five percent of all plan sponsors are unaware of or unfamiliar with 'hidden' costs and fees embedded in their plan, despite ERISA requirements that they ensure such fees are reasonable, a new study by Investmart found." "Managing 401(k) Plans," Institute of Management & Administration (IOMA), December 1, 2001.

   "The Department of Labor's 1998 'Study of 401(k) Plan Fees and Expenses' revealed that nearly 80% of plan sponsors didn't know how much their plans cost." "Confusion Reigns When It Comes to 401k Plan Fees," Roxanne Fleszar, 401kWire, July 26, 1999

   http://www.financial-management.com/planfees.html

3. "A Look at 401(k) Plan Fees," U.S. Department of Labor Pension and Welfare Benefits Administration, 1998, p. 2.

4. Whose Board?
   If directors of mutual fund companies redefined their role, shareholders would benefit
   —John C. Bogle is the chairman of the Vanguard Group.

   Managers' profits have grown even faster. Despite their pervasive failure to out-perform the market, many fund managers are now booking pretax profit margins of 35 to 40 percent. And margins of probably 50 to 60 percent exist before factoring in marketing costs—costs that benefit fund managers by increasing assets and fees but that are borne by the fund shareholders.
   http://www.bloomberg.com/personal/archives/vcs_A9712_bog.html

5. "That 401(k) May Cost More Than You Think," Jeffrey Laderman, *Business Week,* November 10, 1997, p. 130.

6. "Protect Yourself Against Retirement Rip-Off," *Money,* April 1997, p. 98

7. "A Look at 401(k) Plan Fees," U.S. Department of Labor Pension and Welfare Benefits Administration, 1998, p. 2.

8. "How to Protect Yourself Against the Great Retirement Rip-off," by Penelope Wang, *Money,* April '97
    http://www.timyounkin.com/periodicals.html

    According to Spectrem Group's projections, the aggregate 401(k) marketplace generates $13.204 billion of total fees, of which 89.5 percent ($11.817 billion) is derived from asset fees, while the remaining 10.5 percent ($1.387 billion) comes from service fees. "Plan Sponsors Need Better Fix on 401(k) Fees," *Employee Benefit Plan Review,* September 2001, p. 22.

9. "How Funds Get Rich at your Expense", *Money Magazine,* February 1995.

10. ". . . today's employees are a litigious bunch. If they ever bear the brunt of a long and painful bear market for stocks, you may find yourself in court trying to explain why you, as a fiduciary, ignored the damage done to employee's retirement security by sky-high plan costs." "Facing Up to Total Plan Costs," *CFO,* April 1996, p. 1.

11. "Economics of Defined Contribution Plans," speech given by Kevin Weise, American Express Retirement Services, March 24, 1998.

12. Administrative fees are often paid by the plan sponsor. Increasingly, however, employers are passing part or all of this cost to participants.

    What You Pay for 401(k)s
    By Jane Bryant Quinn
    Thursday, January 8, 1998
    Copyright 1998 Washington Post Writer's Group
    http://retireplan.about.com/gi/dynamic/offsite.htm?site=http%3A%2F%2Fwww.washingtonpost.com%2Fwp-srv%2Fbusiness%2Flongterm%2Fquinn%2Fcolumns%2F010898.htm

Sponsors must be careful as to which expenses can be properly transferred to plan participants. In Advisory Opinion 2001-01A, issued in January 2001, "the DOL . . . stated that the key element in deciding if costs can be paid from plan assets is identifying an expense as a 'settlor' expense (related to establishing, designing, or terminating a plan) or a 'fiduciary' one, such as those resulting from the operation and administration of the plan. . . . Settlor expenses such as choosing what type of qualified plan to offer employees, preparing the plan documents, plan amendments to add new features, etc. may not be paid for by the plan. . . . Fiduciary expenses such as amendments to comply with tax law changes, calculations of benefits for participants, routine nondiscrimination testing, preparation of Form 5500, administering the loan program and communicating plan information to participants and beneficiaries may be eligible for payment from plan assets." "Plan Expenses: Can They Be Paid from Plan Assets?" *Plan Sponsor Outlook*, 2nd quarter 2001, The Guardian Life Insurance Company.

13. According to Spectrem Group's projections, the aggregate 401(k) marketplace generates $13.204 billion of total fees, of which 89.5 percent ($11.817 billion) is derived from asset fees, while the remaining 10.5 percent ($1.387 billion) comes from service fees. "Plan Sponsors Need Better Fix on 401(k) Fees," *Employee Benefit Plan Review*, September 2001, p. 22.

14. After a while of looking at various leading bundled provider's product, you begin to see the same "outside" funds over and over again (e.g., AIM, Dodge & Cox, Janus, Pimco, etc.). There is a simple reason for this, and, in a word, it's distribution. These are fund families who have made the strategic business decision to sell their product as "investment only" (as opposed to creating a fully bundled product as a means to distribute product). They make sure their product is part of the investment platform of the large bundled providers, who, in turn, collect a fee for distribution.

According to Cerulli Associates, investment-only 401(k) assets will exceed 401(k) proprietary assets by 2006.

Source: Speech made by a Consultant from Cerulli Associates, Inc. at the Scudder Investments Consultant Symposium held on February 1, 2002 in Key Biscayne, FL—Slide 26

15. The alliance platform is the "store," which provides "shelf space" to various invest-
    ment companies' "products." In exchange for the "shelf space," the product
    providers pay for this service when their product is bought.

16. "401(k)'s Dirty Little Secret," *Bloomberg Personal,* September 1997, p. 4.

17. "12-1 fees, charged by some funds, are deducted from the plan assets to pay mar-
    keting and advertising expenses or, more commonly, to compensate sales profes-
    sionals. By law, 12b-1 fees cannot exceed 0.75 percent of the fund's average net
    assets per year. The fund may also charge a service fee of up to .25 percent of averge
    net assets per year to compensate sales professionals."
    The Mutual Fund Business, Robert C. Pozen, The MIT Press, 1998, p. 20.

    "From a relative handful of funds adopting the charges in the mid-1980s, some 70
    percent of funds today have 12b-1 fees in place, according to data from
    Morningstar. . . . The impact of 12b-1 fees has helped drive up the overall annual
    fees charged by mutual funds. Between 1979 and 1999, the average expense ratio
    charged by mutual funds increased to 1.36 percent, from 1.14 percent, according to
    a report on mutual fund fees released last year by the SEC. While front-end sales
    loads decreased, the 12b-1 fee was listed as one of the main reasons annual fund
    expenses had risen."
    "Fund Fees Get SEC Scrutiny," Aaron Lucchetti, *Wall Street Journal,* p. C1, May
    28, 2002

18. "Revenue Sharing Aspects of Qualified Retirement Plan Management," Daniel
    Clark, *Solutions,* September 1998, p. 36.

19. Front- and back-end loads, as well as 12b-1 fees, are used to pay intermediaries to
    distribute product. Since Vanguard does not use brokers to distribute its product,
    there are no loads and no 12b-1 fees.

20. A guaranteed investment contract or guaranteed income contract, is a contract
    between an insurance company and a corporate profit-sharing or pension plan (i.e.
    401(k) plan), whereby the plan invests a sum of money with the insurance compa-
    ny for a specified period of time, and the insurance company, in turn, pays interest

on the loan at a fixed rate over the life of the contract. The borrowed funds are then invested by the insurance company in a portfolio of securities, including bonds, mortgages, and are usually structured to mature around the time that the GIC is scheduled to expire.

21. To determine an average expense ratio, sum the expense ratios (and any additional asset-based fee if applicable) of all the investment options and divide by the number found in the portfolio. For example, the sum of .75, 1.0 and 1.25 is 3 percent. The average expense ratio is therefore 100 basis points or, 1 percent. For greater accuracy, you can create an asset-weighted expense ratio by multiplying the expense ratio of each fund by the proportion of the assets of a particular fund to the plan's total assets and sum the number. For example, assume fund 1 has 10 percent of total plan assets and costs .75 percent, fund 2 has 50 percent of total plan assets and costs 1 percent and fund 3 has 40 percent of total plan assets and costs 1.25 percent. The asset-weighted expense ratio would be 108 basis points or, 1.08 percent $[(.10 \times .75) + (.50 \times 1) + (.40 \times 1.25)]$

22. Many of the large mutual fund companies have created retirement share classes which are lower priced alternatives to the higher cost retail version of their funds. Typically these share classes are for mid and large size plans (at least $50 million of plan assets) although if institutional share classes are available, you should ask for them.

CHAPTER 12

A GOOD PLAN
(BENCHMARKING)

✦

Wouldn't it be nice to know how your plan stacks up, whether it's "successful," or, if you don't have a plan yet, to know the answer to the question "What does a 'good' plan look like?" The focus of this chapter is on describing the characteristics of a successful 401(k) plan.

Measuring success presupposes benchmarks against which plans can be compared. Benchmarking is an effective method for examining different aspects of a company's performance. Consultants routinely benchmark companies' various processes, from manufacturing to finance and customer service, in order to determine their competitiveness. The value of a good benchmarking study lies in making comparisons with an established standard. Think of it as a "report card" identifying good and poor performers relative to the benchmark, as well as identifying the factors that contribute to performance differences. With a benchmarking study in hand, management can decide what steps are necessary for improvement.

The idea behind benchmarking a 401(k) plan is simple.[1] By using unbiased criteria to measure a plan, the sponsor can get an accurate measure of its relative strengths and weaknesses. Management then has a powerful tool with which to make informed decisions about improving the plan in such areas as plan design, investments, costs, communication and education strategies, and, finally, service provider competitiveness. Management can also use the information to negotiate more-favorable service and pricing agreements with vendors.

A GOOD PLAN

Just as a routine physical can give you an indication of your general state of health, a review of your plan's essential criteria will give you a sense of the overall quality of your plan. To know if you have a "good" plan, to know whether your plan is "successful," you must ask the following questions and then compare the answers against national normative and industry-specific data:

+ Is the plan in compliance?
+ What is the participation rate?
+ What is the savings rate?
+ Are plan assets allocated appropriately, on the basis of employee demographics?
+ How well have the investments performed in absolute and relative terms?
+ Is the plan cost- and operationally efficient?

In general, the more strictly the plan is administered according to the terms of the plan document; the greater the number of employees who participate in it; the more money they put into it; the better the investment returns; the easier it is to run; and the less costly it is, the more successful the plan. Let me discuss each of these points in more detail.

+ **Compliance**—A successful 401(k) plan is first and foremost in compliance. This means that it is administered exactly as the plan document is written, it completes all necessary testing and government filings and distributes all legally required information to participants. No plan can maintain its qualified status without complying with all relevant ERISA and IRS code sections. (In chapter 4, we have discussed the rules for plan qualification, discrimination testing, and other testing issues.)

✦ **Participation**—This is the litmus test for a successful plan. If nobody is in the plan, it's not working. Average participation rates vary by industry and wage levels. White-collar industries, for example, tend to have higher participation rates than blue-collar and service industries like retail, hospitality, and health care. The more people in a plan the greater the employees' awareness of this important benefit and the easier it is to pass the required testing. (In chapter 10, we have discussed proven methods for raising participation.)

✦ **Average Deferral Percentage**—After you convince employees to enroll in the plan, you should work to encourage higher levels of saving. As a nation, we are habitually low savers, and most people have no idea how much money they will need for retirement. The more money people put aside in their 401(k), the greater their chance for a secure retirement. Also, the higher the savings' rate, the easier it is to pass discrimination testing. (In chapter 10, we have discussed how to raise a group's savings rate.)

✦ **Asset Allocation**—A 401(k) is fundamentally a long-term savings and retirement plan. The difference between a 6 percent, 8 percent, and 10 percent rate of return over a twenty-, thirty-, and forty-year time period can be enormous.[2] Asset allocation, or the relative percentage a participant puts into cash, bonds, and stock, is the fundamental investment decision and can have a huge impact on the funds available at retirement. A frequently heard complaint from plan sponsors is that participants do not invest appropriately given their retirement time horizon.

✦ **Investment Performance**—How well (or poorly) the investment options perform, in both absolute and relative terms, has an obvious impact on participants' account balances. For example, at any given point in time, certain asset classes perform better/worse than others but that doesn't mean the investments have performed poorly. Plan sponsors need to know how well their investments have performed against best-fit indices as well as against other similar funds on a risk-adjusted basis. Cost is another essential ingredient of the investment equation, with lower-cost funds draining away less from participants' accounts. Again, this requires benchmarking and continual monitoring. (In chapter 9, we have discussed how to evaluate, select, and monitor investments.)

✦ **Cost and Administrative Efficiency**—When you are a plan fiduciary, one of your primary responsibilities is determining the "reasonableness" of fees. This presupposes two things: first, that you understand your plan's total cost structure, and second, that you can put these costs into some kind of context of "high," "low," or "average." You can pay a lot and get a little, or you can pay a modest amount and get a lot. The reality is that 401(k)s are primarily participants' money, and since the participants shoulder the majority of plan costs, your primary duty is to keep costs in line. (Chapter 11 is about 401(k) pricing.) In addition, the plan should be run as administratively efficiently as possible. Ideally, the plan participant should be able to communicate directly with the service provider for all routine interactions such as questions about the plan, initiating loans, changing investment options, etc. Plan sponsors should also be able to expect accurate recordkeeping, competent administration, and real-time access to aggregate plan information. (Chapter 8 is about recordkeeping.)

OTHER BENCHMARKING CRITERIA

In addition to the primary criteria above, there are some secondary points to examine when performing a benchmarking study. They are secondary issues not because they aren't important, but because a plan that is successful on the first six criteria, will generally not have problems in these areas. These secondary areas also tend to be more qualitative in nature.

+ **Plan Design**—Ideally, plan design should express and reinforce corporate goals and culture. Such questions as retirement plan type, definition of compensation, eligibility, enrollment dates, and the type and amount of employer contributions, can exert a powerful influence on the overall success or failure of a plan.

+ **Recordkeeping and Plan Technology**—Generally speaking, a plan that is accurate and administratively efficient is built on a robust technology platform. The integration of a toll-free voice response system, a live call center, and a fully transactional Internet, to create a seamless multimedia, multichannel delivery system will go a long way to reduce a company's administrative burden as well as raise the visibility of the plan. For plans with multisite, multistate locations, it is a necessary precondition for success.

+ **Employee Education**—Quality materials available in multiple media formats are essential for communicating basic plan information and educating participants on fundamentals of retirement planning. Participants need information to make informed decisions. Some also require the assistance of advice providers.

• **Vendor Profile**—Although there are several hundred 401(k) service providers to choose from, relatively few have the scale (measured in terms of both participants and assets) to compete effectively in the long run. It takes tremendous commitment—as measured by capital, technology, and people—for service providers to stay competitive. As a buyer this doesn't mean "biggest is best," but it does mean knowing how your service provider stacks up against its competitors in terms of size, scale and commitment.

• **Employee Survey**—What do employees think about the plan? What are their needs, and is the current plan meeting them? How can the plan be improved? If you choose to poll the employees, keep the survey short and focused.

These points will give you a model for quickly evaluating your plan against national data. Benchmarking also provides a paper trail and demonstrates that the plan sponsor regularly examines the critical components of the plan. This could be useful in the future to demonstrate procedural due diligence.

RATING YOUR PLAN: BASIC BENCHMARKING STATISTICS[3]

Below you will find a brief list of some important benchmarking information. Please note that this is not an exhaustive list, and you may have to do some additional work yourself. (For example, you will have to analyze your investments for cost and performance, or hire an adviser to do it for you. See the the appendix for a list of useful resources.) But it should help you understand how your plan stacks up.

+ **Plan compliance**—Plan documents must be up to date and easily accessible. All the appropriate discrimination tests must be conducted and the necessary government forms filed. All of the appropriate disclosure documents must be distributed to plan participants.

+ **Participation**—Varies by plan size and industry category but the overall average is 73 percent.[4]

+ **Average Deferral Percentage**—Varies by gender and industry category. The average highly compensated employee (HCE) deferral rate for women is 7 percent and for men 6.3 percent. The average non–highly compensated employee (NHCE) deferral rate for women is 6.6 percent and for men it's 6.7 percent.[5] Overall, the average participant contributes 6.8 percent of salary on a pre-tax basis and this jumps to 10 percent in plans offering employer matching contributions.[6]

✦ **Average account balance**—Varies by plan size with large (10,000+ employees) plans' average balance of $66,000 much larger than small plans' (0 – 49 employees) average balance of $34,000. The national average is $55,000.

✦ **Asset allocation**—For plans with less than five hundred employees, 7 percent of the assets are in short-term investments, 5 percent in stable value, 4 percent in fixed income, 11 percent in blended, 64 percent in domestic equity, 5 percent in international, and 1 percent in company stock. For plans with between 500 and 2,499 employees, 7 percent of the assets are in short-term investments, 9 percent in stable value, 3 percent in fixed income, 9 percent in blended, 60 percent in domestic equity, 4 percent in international, and 6 percent in company stock.

✦ **Investments**—The average number of investment options available is 12, with large plans (10,000+ employees) offering the most (38) and small plans (0–49 employees) offering the fewest (9). The use of self-directed brokerage accounts has increased 75 percent over the last year, and is now offered in 14 percent of the plans surveyed.[7] Plan assets were most commonly managed by mutual funds (43.8 percent), banks (15.5 percent), insurance companies (13.2 percent), investment advisors (10.3 percent), and brokerage firms (8.9 percent).[8]

✦ **Plan design**

1. **Eligibility**—37 percent use immediate eligibility, 13.2 percent use three months, 15.3 percent use six months or a thousand hours, 25.1 percent use one year, and 9.4 percent use "Other."[9]

2. **Company Contributions**—The average company contribution was 4.6 percent of payroll. Company contributions were highest in profit-sharing plans (8.2 percent) of payroll and lowest in 401(k) plans (2.5 percent). Company contributions averaged 22.6 percent of total net profit for profit-sharing plans and 11.8 percent of total net profit for 401(k) plans.[10]

3. **Vesting**—37 percent of all plans report immediate vesting, 46 percent have graded vesting, and the remaining 17 percent have cliff vesting.[11]

4. **Loans**—90 percent of participants have access to loans. 81 percent of participants have no loans, 14 percent have one loan, 4 percent have two loans, and 1 percent have three loans. On average, in plans that permit loans, 19.4 percent of participants have loans, averaging $6,309 per borrower. Loans accounted for 2 percent of total plan assets in plans permitting loans.[12]

✦ **Plan costs**

The table below shows average plan costs for different sized plans. (Data taken from *401(k) Averages Plan Book*.)

	25 participants; $1,000,000 in assets	50 participants; $2,000,000 in assets	100 participants; $4,000,000 in assets	200 participants; $8,000,000 in assets
Average plan cost per participant	$637.60	$583.14	$560.59	$525.63
Average plan cost as a percentage of assets	Investment: 1.30% Record-keeping/ Administration: .24% Trustee: .05% Total Bundled: 1.59%	Investment: 1.26% Record-keeping/ Administration: .17% Trustee: .03% Total Bundled: 1.46%	Investment: 1.26% Record-keeping/ Administration: .13% Trustee: .01% Total Bundled: 1.40%	Investment: 1.20% Record-keeping/ Administration: .10% Trustee: .01% Total Bundled: 1.31%
Range of total plan costs	Low: $10,151 Average: $15,757 High: $23,781	Low: $16,900 Average: $29,053 High: $46,461	Low: $30,061 Average: $55,796 High: $90,621	Low: $47,330 Average: $104,772 High: $178,940

✦ **Technology**

 1. **Daily valuation**—Participants direct the investment of their own contributions in 100 percent of the plans surveyed, their employer's matching contribution in 80 percent of plans surveyed, and the profit-sharing contributions in 85 percent of plans surveyed.[13]

 2. **Internet**—Seventy-nine percent of plans permit participants to make some kind of transaction via the Internet.

401(k) PITFALLS

Now that we've looked at what constitutes "success," let's examine what constitutes "failure." Just as certain attributes define "successful" plans, "failed" plans usually share common characteristics.

 1. Not setting up a retirement plan
If at all possible, every company should set up a retirement plan, especially small businesses where only a small percentage offer one.[14] There is a retirement plan design for just about every company. You owe it to yourself and to your employees to start one. Cost should not be an issue, since, as we saw in chapter 2, a distinguishing feature of 401(k) plans is that they do not require an employer contribution. When small businesses compete for talent, they put themselves at a real disadvantage by not offering a retirement plan.[15]

 2. Not understanding how the plan works in advance
If you don't understand 401(k) basics, you may be in for a surprise when the plan faces its annual compliance tests. Without a proper understanding of retirement plan basics, you may overlook other, more attractive plan design options, like age-weighted

or integrated profit sharing, SIMPLE, or safe-harbor 401(k) alternatives. You might also dismiss plan features like employer-matching contributions too quickly.

3. Underestimating employees' capacity to save and understand

Many employers underestimate the capacity and willingness of their employees to save and invest. Remember, 401(k) is fundamentally employees' money. Most people care about their retirement, and if the benefits, costs, and risks of participating are properly explained, they will respond enthusiastically.

4. Not setting overall plan goals

What does a good plan look like? How does your plan stack up against relevant standards? A proper diagnosis of the plan's condition will go a long way toward understanding the plan's overall condition and will help in the vendor selection process.

5. Not understanding the true cost of the plan

When most plan-buyers look at costs, they see only the explicit fees of the plan. This is misleading, and misses the "implicit" costs embedded in the investments. As we saw in chapter 11, vendors earn most of their fees off of the investments. Plan buyers often don't understand or don't question these fees. When you don't examine the investment side of the cost equation, you compromise your ability to judge the reasonableness of fees.

6. Not holding vendors to higher standards

Effective business today means partnering, and that includes your service provider. Set mutually agreed-upon goals, specifying realistic time frames and consequences if they are not met. The likelihood of meeting plan goals increases dramatically if everyone agrees on what they are. Finally, measure the results on a regular basis using before-and-after data, perhaps in an annual stewardship report.

7. *Not giving the plan top management support and regulating the plan to obscurity*

A plan does not become successful by itself. You don't just start it and put it on autopilot. Success requires the care, support, and attention of senior management. As your company changes over time, the plan will also need to change. And if you don't pay attention to the plan, it can fall into neglect and disrepair. Of course, it's in top management's best interests to encourage the plan, since the ability of the top managers to save is linked to the savings rate of the NHCEs.

8. *Not understanding how vital education is to the long-term success of the plan*

Helping employees make informed decisions about their retirement is critical to the success of a plan and to the ability of employees to reach their retirement goals. With the decline in traditional defined benefit plans, as well as the uncertainty about Social Security, workers are increasingly responsible for their retirement. But the facts don't bode well. Many people don't save enough and are ignorant of basic financial concepts. Plan sponsors are often the last best hope for employees.

9. *No Investment Policy Statement and no ongoing monitoring*

Investments are the engines that drive retirement accumulation balances. Not having a systematic process for the selection and monitoring of investment performance is like not regularly servicing your car: performance will suffer and eventually it will break down. Not only is this bad for your employees, but as a fiduciary you are held to a much higher standard of behavior and your inaction can be grounds for a lawsuit.

Now that we've examined each of the main pieces of a 401(k) plan and know what a good plan looks like, it's time to put our knowledge to work and select a provider.

Notes

1. There is a lot of information about retirement plans in general and 401(k) plans in particular. The problem is that the information is spread out and time-consuming to accumulate. When I became a consultant in this business, the first thing I did was compile quality information from different sources to create a benchmarking template.

2. One dollar invested at year-end 1925 would have grown to the following amounts by year-end 2001:

   + Inflation—$9.86
   + Treasury Bills—$17.20
   + Long-Term Government Bonds—$50.66
   + Large company stocks—$2,279.13
   + Small company stocks—$7,860.05

   Stocks, Bonds, Bills, and Inflation, Ibbotson Associates, Inc., 2001

3. All of the data from this section, unless otherwise noted, comes from "Building Futures, Volume III: How Workplace Savings are Shaping the Future of Retirement," *Fidelity Investments, 2001.*

4. According to the Profit Sharing Council of America's 44th Annual Survey, participation is 80.2 percent.

5. According the Profit Sharing Council of America's 44th Annual Survey, HCEs contributed 6.4 percent and NHCEs contributed 5.3 percent of their wages.

6. "Studies Examine Average 401(k) Plan Contribution, Year-End Asset Allocation," *Retirement Plan Trends*, AUL, February 2002.

7. Morgan Stanley Dean Witter Investment Management 2000 Survey of the 401(k) Market.

8. Profit Sharing Council of America's 44th Annual Survey.

9. "Table 3: 401(k) Plan Eligibility Type by Company Size," 401(k) and Profit-sharing plan Eligibility Survey 2001, Profit Sharing/401(k) Council of America, p. 3.

10. Profit Sharing Council of America's 44th Annual Survey.

11. "Eligibility, Vesting Requirements Getting Looser," data compiled from William M. Mercer's 2000–2001 Survey on Employee Savings Plans, *www.PlanSponsor.com*, December 27, 2001.

12. Profit Sharing Council of America's 44th Annual Survey.

13. "Participants Direct Most Plan Investments," *www.PlanSponsor.com*, December 27, 2001.

14. According to The Pension & Welfare Benefits Administration, small businesses employ nearly 40% of the private-sector workforce in the United States. However, a majority of small businesses do not offer their workers retirement savings benefits. *http://www.acctsite.com/articles/retirementoptionssmallbus.htm*

   Percentage of Businesses Offering Various Types of Benefits to Their Full Time Employees:

   + Retirement Plan/401K 28%
   + Profit-sharing plan 15%

   http://entrepreneurs.about.com/library/weekly/aa071900b.htm

15. "Faced with the choice between two similar jobs, one with excellent retirement benefits that meets their minimum salary requirements and another with a higher salary but poor retirement benefits, workers in companies with 10 to 500 employees tend to say they would choose the job with the excellent retirement benefits (57%) rather than the higher salary (37%)." Transamerica Retirement Survey 2001, prepared by Mathew Greenwald & Associates, Inc., October 2001, p. 12.

CHAPTER 13

PUTTING IT ALL TOGETHER

VENDOR SELECTION

Y̲ou're finally ready to choose a service provider. But whether you're going to start up a new retirement plan or change one or all of the vendors currently servicing your plan, you'll need more than just information to do it right. There's reams of data out there (not necessarily arranged in a coherent way.) Where do you start? You need a process, a way to sort through what can appear to be an overwhelming number of options.[1]

This chapter is about bringing the vendor-selection process together into a logical, cohesive whole. It is the "how-to" chapter, designed as a step-by-step process, to guarantee that you make the right buying decision for your company.

One of the themes stressed throughout this book is that your fiduciary responsibility is intimately linked to procedural due diligence. In the last analysis, you demonstrate diligence through process, not outcome. With 401(k)s increasingly in the headlines, you cannot afford to be careless when selecting service providers or picking investments. There's just too much at stake, both for you and your employees. Following a systematic, rigorous process and documenting each step is necessary for two reasons. First, it will increase the chances of making a correct buying decision. Second, it will ensure that the actions you take to select a vendor can be defended. Remember, when you are the steward of other people's money, your actions are held to a very high standard. So, let's get started. Your employees are counting on you.

The buying process can be broken down into several discrete steps, each one contributing to the overall integrity of the process. As with any large project involving a lot of information, the key to successful selection and implementation is time. Give yourself enough time to do the job correctly. You don't want to have to repeat this process any time soon if you don't have to. Below you'll find a brief overview of the eleven steps that will help you find the best service provider for your company.

MARKETING PROCESS OVERVIEW

1. Benchmark the Current Plan

If you already have a plan, it's important to know how it stacks up against key benchmarks: compliance, participation, average deferral percentage, asset allocation, investment performance, and plan costs. A thorough understanding of the current plan's strengths and weaknesses will help to determine if "marketing" the plan (i.e., shopping the plan to other service providers) is even necessary. It may be that the plan's weaknesses have more to do with plan design, employee demographics, or lack of company focus than vendor performance.[2]

If you do decide that vendor performance is part of the problem and that marketing is necessary, a benchmarking analysis will identify plan weaknesses. This will, in turn, become the starting point for setting well-defined goals. You may also wish to survey employees and ask them for their opinions of the plan and what they would like to see improved. Armed with this information, you are now ready to begin the marketing process.

2. Determine the Decision-Making Body

Decide who will be part of the decision-making team. A small committee of people from different parts of the organization (finance, human resources, operations, management, legal) is usually best. If there are "vocal" employees who have been advocating change, perhaps this is the time to bring them into the process too. By making a group decision, you will ensure support from key personnel—an asset in selling the plan throughout the organization. To avoid any last-minute power struggles, make sure that the committee has final decision-making power. You may also conclude that an internal committee does not have the resources to conduct a thorough search and that you need assistance in specific areas. We now look at the pros and cons of hiring outsiders to assist in the project.

3. Hire an Outsider

Does it make sense to hire a third-party to assist with the vendor selection process, new plan installation, and/or investment monitoring process? You may decide that, collectively, your company doesn't have the time or expertise to perform these tasks by itself. More and more small and mid-size companies are following the lead of large companies and hiring consultants to assist them in the search process. Small companies have always relied on outside help, usually through accountants, insurance agents, and general benefit brokers. Specialized experts (whether they are brokers or consultants) can provide invaluable assistance by bringing speed, objectivity, organizational efficiency, and negotiating power to the process. But hiring an outsider does not necessarily guarantee a good buying decision. Here are some key questions to ask:

+ *What are the broker's/consultant's qualifications?*
   Is he a pension expert or a benefit generalist? How many vendor searches has he conducted? Who are his clients? Can you talk to them? Does he understand investments, recordkeeping, compliance, employee education and communication? Insist on seeing work samples. Does the broker/consultant follow a systematic and thorough process? Can he do everything you want done? Will you receive written documentation highlighting the

main facts of the evaluation and selection process? Is the broker/consultant objective? Does he have any formal marketing relationships that may influence his recommendation? How quickly can he complete the project? Does he have support staff to help? Who will negotiate performance and service standards: you or the broker/consultant?

✦ *How does the broker/consultant get paid: fee or commission?*
If you are a start-up or "small" plan (generally speaking, under $25 million in total plan assets), there are many good bundled 401(k) products that have commissions built into them and are designed to be distributed by "brokers," i.e., third-party intermediaries who are remunerated for their services. To complicate matters, there are other good products that do not have commissions built into them. If you do use a broker, do not expect him to bring a noncommissioned product to you. If you prefer to use a consultant and pay a fee instead, insist on a "scope of services" agreement detailing exactly what the consultant will do and how and when he will be paid. To protect the integrity of the process and to avoid any conflicts of interest, you need to know in advance exactly how the third-party gets paid.

4. Set Plan Objectives and Goals

It is important to understand what you want to achieve prior to starting. Setting goals dictates the nature of the search and simplifies it immensely. Setting goals first, rather than relying on the search process to define them, will dramatically improve the speed and quality of the vendor search process. If you already have a plan, benchmark it! If no plan currently exists, write down overall objectives based on the data in this book. By clarifying plan objectives in advance, you automatically narrow the dizzying array of potential service providers to a manageable number, say, five to ten, and greatly simplify the search process.

5. Select Markets

The next step is to "pick markets" (i.e., decide from which service providers you would like to get a proposal.) Ask companies similar to yours whom they use and why they like or dislike the vendor. Consult media sources (See the appendix). *CFO* and *Plan Sponsor Magazine* print annual 401(k) "buying guides." I usually try to select at least one provider from each of the main vendor types—bank, insurance company, brokerage firm, and mutual fund company—for comparison purposes. Depending on overall goals, plan design complexity, asset size, employee demographics, geographic location, and company culture, you will naturally gravitate toward certain types of service provider configurations (e.g., bundled, alliance, unbundled, etc.) and certain types of vendors (e.g., mutual fund, bank, insurance company, etc.) For example, a five-hundred-employee white-collar company spread out in several locations across the country with $15 million in plan assets and a straightforward plan design may end up looking at more bundled, mutual fund–based products.

6. Draft an Investment Policy Statement (IPS)

If you don't already have one, drafting an IPS will also simplify the search process. Even if you only decide on core asset classes, the total number of funds, and the number of funds in each class, these steps will go a long way toward allowing comparisons across different service providers' investment universes. Once you pick your service provider, a well-designed IPS will also prevent you from becoming overwhelmed by the investment selection process. (For more information about IPS, see chapter 9, "Investments," and the appendix.)

7. Send out a Request for Proposal (RFP)

A well-written RFP is the backbone of a good search. Without one, it is difficult to conduct a diligent search. An RFP also saves time by allowing you to ask core capability questions in a structured format and to cross-reference answers from a broad spectrum of good-fit service providers. A good RFP should contain all of the following sections:

+ *Plan information*
Basic plan information, such as assets broken down by investment option, eligible and participating employees, locations, net annual cash flow, payroll, plan design, etc. Service providers need all relevant information about your plan so they can respond in detail. Withholding key information from service providers during the marketing process is counterproductive.

+ *Goals and search objectives*
Tell the potential service providers exactly what you are trying to accomplish. By letting them know your goals early on in the RFP stage, you will help them to address your needs better.

+ *Detailed questionnaire*
All key areas, such as provider overview, compliance, record-keeping and administration, investments, employee education materials, implementation schedule, and fees, should be addressed.

If you are in a hurry, there are several high-quality Web sites where you can both shop for a plan and indeed, buy one. If you are setting up a plan for the first time, the shopping sites allow for easy vendor comparisons. They can take the place of an RFP, since few service providers will respond to a full-blown RFP request from a start-up plan. If you already have a plan, these sites can be a useful way to quickly gather good information about service providers, but they lack the detailed responses and customized nature of a properly completed RFP response. See the appendix for more information about RFPs and web-based shopping sites.

8. Analyze Vendor Responses

Now that you have collected all the data, it's time to analyze it. There are many criteria by which to evaluate service providers: record-keeping/

administration, investments, education, costs, compliance services and market share, to name just a few. Some things, like recordkeeping functionality, technological features, investment performance, and plan costs, are quantifiable and lend themselves readily to spreadsheet analysis. (We discussed these areas in detail in chapters 9, 10, and 12.) Others, like the quality of employee education materials and commitment to service, are more subjective. This is where a well-designed RFP is invaluable, since it will give you a good idea of a vendor's true strengths and weaknesses. For example, the ability of the vendor to meet your company's needs in areas like outsourcing, merger and acquisition services, and ongoing education and communication are often critical to the success of a plan and should be factored into the capabilities of a 401(k) provider. Depending on your search objectives, you may wish to weight certain areas more than others and rank the vendors by a point system.

9. Select Finalists and Interview

The reason for the analysis is to select the best vendor for your needs. Once you make your preliminary selections, you will want to contact the finalists and ask them to come in for a brief, well-structured interview. (As a courtesy, you should notify the RFP respondents who did not make the final cut of your decision as quickly as possible.) Because salespeople can be long-winded, for the sake of efficiency, it is a good idea to establish the parameters of the meeting in advance. Prior to the interviews, I send an agenda to the finalists so that they come prepared. A typical agenda includes the following information:

- ✦ Meeting dates and time allowed
- ✦ Names and titles of people in attendance
- ✦ Restatement of plan search and objectives
- ✦ Suggested outline of the meeting: recordkeeping and administration, investments, employee education, costs and fees, conversion process, etc.

The point of the meeting is to have the company representative paint a detailed picture of how their systems work, how they would help your plan meet its overall goals, and to review important information about fees, timelines, responsibilities, etc.

By analyzing the finalists' RFP responses and conducting a cost- and hypothetical-investment analysis in advance,[3] you can keep the meetings brief and to the point. The agenda will also keep everyone on track. If appropriate, you may also request that finalists bring the actual people with whom you will be working during the transition and on a day-to-day basis once the plan is firmly established. That way, you can meet the vendor's service team in advance, to determine if there are any compatibility issues.

Finally, if time and budget permit, try to visit the recordkeeping facility of your top one or two finalists to meet the people who will administer your plan back at the "home office." There is nothing quite like taking a behind-the-scenes tour of a service provider's administrative shop. This is also a good time to "kick" the technology tires of the finalists. Visiting the call center, seeing the technology that supports the plan in action, and meeting the people who are responsible for administering your plan, is highly recommended.

10. Check References and Read Service Agreements

After you have conducted in-person interviews and on site meetings, call the references you requested in the RFP. Asking a combination of specific and open-ended questions will get you better responses. Try to contact at least one client that has recently left the vendor. Recently terminated clients often have a different perspective than current ones.

Now is also the time to request a plan service agreement so you can see what services are included and which are guaranteed. At a minimum, it should include responsibility for payroll data, participant statements and sponsor reports, all required discrimination testing and preparation of SPDs and a signature-ready 5500.

11. Select Vendor and Negotiate Contracts

You're almost finished. It's time to pick the vendor. Now is your best chance of securing the most favorable pricing. As in most business ventures, the more money you bring to the table (both in gross dollars as well as average account balances), the greater your ability to negotiate a better deal. Things you might want to consider requesting:

+ Waiver of setup and/or conversion costs
+ Increased use of nonproprietary or "outside" funds
+ Reduction in annual explicit fees
+ Reduction in asset-based "wrap" fees, if applicable
+ Use of institutionally priced investment options
+ More employee enrollment meetings, both first year and subsequent years
+ Performance guarantees with some of the vendor's fees "at risk"
+ Vendor commitment to overall plan goals, such as participation, savings rates, and asset allocation

MARKETING SUMMARY

To do a good job, to be procedurally diligent, you are required to take the majority of the above steps. As you review the process, consider whether you and your company have the staff, the time, and the expertise to take these steps by yourselves. If not, consider hiring a qualified professional to assist in some or all of the steps. And remember, give yourself enough time. In the case of start-up plans, that means one to three months. In the case of existing plans, the time needed to conduct a due diligent market search and to transition the plan usually is four to eight months.

TRANSFERRING ASSETS AND RECORDS: WAYS TO MINIMIZE THE "BLACKOUT" PERIOD

If you already have a plan set up, moving a plan from one service provider to another can be a time-consuming and exasperating experience. There are simple ways to minimize the inevitable headaches.

Transferring records and assets involves dealing with four main issues:

1. The correct valuation of the assets maintained by the old recordkeeper and trustee
2. The correct transfer of participant account information from the old to the new recordkeeper
3. The establishment of participant account information by the new recordkeeper
4. The communication of the entire process to the employees

Once a plan has decided to change providers, it must stop remitting contributions to the old provider at a certain point and start sending them to the new provider. At the same time, the old recordkeeper (who has just been fired) has to properly "value" all of the participant balances as of the transfer date of the assets. During this time, participants have no access either to information about their accounts or to the money in their accounts. This is the infamous "blackout," "lockdown," or "quiet" period. Once the plan balances are finally valued by the old provider, the new recordkeeper who has been preparing to receive the transfer information accepts and reconciles the account balances with the transferred amounts. The new recordkeeper then sends an account statement to each of the participants confirming the correct transfer amount. The amount of data to be transferred and the quality of the records determines how quickly this process can be completed. Generally speaking, the cleaner the data the easier the transfer. There are some vendors who, with quality data and enough time, can execute a seamless conversion and eliminate the blackout period entirely.

SIMPLIFYING THE TRANSFER PROCESS

There are steps you can take prior to transferring records to assist the process. First, you may use the occasion to legally pay out any terminated employees who have an account balance of less than $5,000. Not only will this simplify the transfer, you might also save some money if you are being charged recordkeeping fees for inactive plan participants. Next, clean up any outstanding recordkeeping issues prior to the transfer so that you only move clean data and records. Finally, communicate the entire process to the employees in advance of the conversion. Timely information is the linchpin of a successful conversion. Give participants ample warning of deadlines for moving money between investment options and taking loans and hardship withdrawals. Finally, show them the new fund options and where the old funds will be going.

Once you've successfully implemented your start-up or transitioned your existing plan, it's time to review. Did the plan reach its goals? Plans are not static, and an ongoing review procedure will ensure that the plan stays on track. Review investment performance at least annually. Also, review the critical success measures of the plan at the same time (e.g., compliance, participation, average deferral percentage, asset allocation, etc.) and make changes as necessary.

COMMON MISTAKES IN THE VENDOR SELECTION PROCESS

✦ *Not being procedurally diligent in the search process*
Many sponsors relegate the provider decision to the last minute, don't evaluate investment options, and don't understand costs well enough to make a good, long-term buying decision. This is bad both for the participants and for the company, since it represents a wasted opportunity to provide a top-notch benefit.

✦ *Attempting a market search without the requisite time, personnel or expertise*
You're swamped. It's mid-October. Your assistant is away on an extended leave. You can barely get your own work done when your boss says, "Let's look into starting a 401(k) plan this January." You have no idea where to start or what to look for. You read this book and become concerned about the ramifica-

tions of not making a good buying decision. Part of the answer is to involve colleagues from other parts of the company, such as finance, human resources, and operations, as well as highly motivated or interested employees. Another part of the answer may also involve hiring a third-party broker or consultant to assist.

✦ *Allowing the retirement plan decision-making process to be hijacked by politics and personal relationships*
If there is one company buying decision that should be separated from company politics or other business relationships, it's this one. Evaluate service providers strictly on their ability to meet your employees' retirement needs. Don't select a plan just because your good friend or brother-in-law, who is a part-time insurance agent, has one to sell. This is a bad decision and one that could have lasting legal and financial repercussions.

✦ *Not asking a third-party broker or consultant enough tough questions*
You decide to ask for help in the buying process and turn to the company president's stockbroker or the health insurance agent for assistance. Both of them dabble in the qualified plan business yet neither has actually ever set up a plan or successfully transitioned one. There is no agreement on the services they will perform nor any discussion on how they will be paid.

✦ *Not shopping around*
As in any marketplace, it pays to shop around. Especially since you are buying a product that will support your employees throughout their retirement. That is a serious fiduciary obligation. Different providers with similar service offerings may charge radically different fees.

✦ *Confusing salespeople with consultants and brokers*
Most 401(k) service providers distribute their product through an in-house sales force, and these salespeople are often quite good at

their job, which is selling product. Be careful of relying on them too much for objective information. They may not know the state of the marketplace or other, better alternatives. In addition, they may not be qualified to help you select investments and draft a written investment policy statement.

✦ *Reducing the buying decision to only cost*
  Cost is an important part of the 401(k) buying decision, but it is not the only one. Costs need to be placed in a context of the type and quality of the overall services received. And investment-related charges need to be placed into a context of risk-adjusted returns over an extended market period. To base the selection decision simply on who has the lowest cost is a short-sighted solution with long-lasting repercussions.

In the end, it all comes down to this: a good process leads to a good result. There is no silver bullet, no single plan design or service provider that is right for every company or even most companies.

I've worked for over ten years in the field, but my consulting practice still relies on the system laid out in this book for selecting and maintaining a retirement plan. Smart choices don't just happen—there are no shortcuts. All the elements—benchmarking, the request for proposal, plan design and investment analysis, employee education and a regular, on-going system for plan evaluation—are vital.

I've put a lot of emphasis on fiduciary responsibility. Documenting your work will leave a clear paper trail and serve as proof that you executed your fiduciary duties with care and diligence. And if you're in over your head, get professional help. But evaluate your advisors carefully—your fiduciary responsibility extends even to your choice of help.

For better or worse, most Americans must now take an active role in planning for their own financially secure retirement. And plan sponsors play a key role in making that goal of security a reality. The last, best thought I can leave you with is also an excellent departure point for any retirement plan search: Your employees are counting on you. Keep that thought front and center. It's the best compass for your trip.

Notes

1. "There are more than 8,000 mutual funds available today (more than the number of publicly traded businesses) and perhaps as many as 200 vendor/product platforms (a platform is a bundled or integrated service encompassing administration, employee communications and education, and investment management) competing in the market for your attention and, ultimately, your business. Add in another 3,000 firms wanting to manage your assets and a host of recordkeepers, administrators, consultants and advisors, and you have the dizzying mix of configurations and approaches confronting today's plan sponsor community." "Revenue Sharing Aspects of Qualified Retirement Plan Management," Daniel Clark, *Solutions,* September 1998, p. 35.

2. This view is corroborated by the Department of Labor's ERISA Advisory Council in their "Report of the Working Group on Guidance in Selecting and Monitoring Service Providers" where they write:

    "Many of the problems with respect to service providers arise because the responsible fiduciary either does not understand his role and responsibility in the selection and monitoring of service providers or exercises poor judgement because he does not have experience or an appropriate source of information concerning legal requirements and industry practices."

    "Selecting Vendors for Your Defined Contribution Plan," Schultz, Collins, Lawso, Chambers, Inc.

3. A hypothetical investment portfolio represents a way in which to assess the overall quality of a particular service provider's investment universe. Using core asset classes such as international equity, large, mid, small cap equity and fixed income, and taking into consideration any restrictions on the ratio of proprietary to nonproprietary funds, one can glean certain insights based on the aggregate portfolio as opposed to looking at funds individually. For example, a well-constructed hypothetical investment portfolio will tell you the average cost of the lineup and also how it has performed as a whole over time. It takes attention away from the performance of a particular fund and instead gives a truer indication of the quality of a service provider's investment universe.

APPENDIX

Retirement Plan Overview

	Contribution Cost to Employer	Employee Elective Deferral Limit	Testing Requirements	Loans	Vesting
Simplified Employee Pension (SEP)	The employer contributes a uniform amount to each participant's IRA up to 25% of compensation, or $40,000 whichever is less	N/A	N/A	Not permitted	100% immediately vested
SIMPLE IRA (for companies with less than 100 employees)	Employer must match up to 3% of the employee's compensation; if the employer chooses to contribute less than 3%, he can give employees proper notice and reduce the contribution to as low as 1%, as long as it is not done for more than two years out of the five year period ending with the year of the reduced contributions. Alternatively, the employer may make a straight 2% contribution for all eligible employees, whether or not they contribute to the plan	Up to $7,000	N/A	Not permitted	100% immediately vested
SIMPLE 401(k) (for companies with less than 100 employees)	Employer matches dollar for dollar up to 3% to all 401(k) participants or a 2% contribution to all eligible employees	Up to $7,000	N/A	Permitted	100% immediately vested
Traditional 401(k)	No employer contribution required	Up to $11,000	ADP & ACP	Permitted	Permitted
Safe Harbor 401(k)	Employer must contribute 3% on behalf of all eligible employees or match 100% of employee contributions up to 3% of compensation plus 50% of employee deferrals in excess of 3% up to 5% of compensation. As an alternative approach, a matching safe harbor contribution can be achieved by making an "enhanced" match, which is dollar for dollar up to the first 4% of compensation	Up to $11,000	N/A	Permitted	100% immediately vested

	Contribution Cost to Employer	Employee Elective Deferral Limit	Testing Requirements	Loans	Vesting
Profit Sharing	Employer has the flexibility to determine the amount of contribution each year up to 25% of eligible compensation or $40,000	N/A	• Coverage • Top-Heavy	Permitted	Permitted
Money Purchase	The employer contributes a *fixed* percentage of compensation to the plan each year, regardless of profits up to 25% of eligible compensation or $40,000	N/A	• Coverage • Top-Heavy	Permitted	Permitted
Target Benefit	The employer makes all contributions to a target benefit plan. The contribution required to fund this benefit on a level basis to retirement age is actuarially determined	N/A	• Coverage • Minimum Funding • Alternative Cross-Testing	Permitted	Permitted
403(b) **(not-for-profit entities)**	No employer contribution required	Up to $11,000	N/A	Permitted	Permitted
457(b)	The company's out-of-pocket expense, notwithstanding matching contributions (if any) and annual administration costs is zero	$11,000—before tax elective deferrals	N/A	Permitted	Permitted

Summary of Plan Changes
Effective in 2002

Plan Provisions—Contributions and deductions Note: Except where indicated, provision is required (** optional provision)	Amendment Required?
IRC Section 415(c)(1) Annual Additions Limit (for 401(k) and other defined contribution plans)—The lesser of $40,000 or 100% of compensation. Future cost-of-living increases will be indexed in $1,000 increments.	Yes
IRC Section 401(a)(17) Compensation Limit—$200,000, with future cost-of-living increases indexed in $5,000 increments.	Yes
IRC Section 402(g)(1) Elective Deferral Limit (for 401(k), 403(b) and 457 plans)—$11,000 to increase in annual $1,000 increments to $15,000 in 2006. Future cost-of-living increases will be rounded in multiples of $500.	No [but must reference Code §402(g)]
Coordination of Deferral Limits between 401(k) Plans and 457 Plans—Beginning in 2002, the deferral limits will no longer need to be coordinated.	No
IRC Section 415(b)(1) Annual Benefits Payable Limit (for defined benefit plans)—$160,000,with future annual cost-of-living increases indexed in $5,000 increments.	Yes
Deductions for Contributions to a Defined Benefit Plan—No deduction is available for contributions that exceed 165% of a plan's current liability, to increase to 170% in 2003 and to be eliminated entirely after 2003 so that the limit will become the excess of accrued liability over asset value.	Yes
Employer Tax Deduction Limit (all defined contribution plans, except as provided by regulations)—25% of compensation of eligible employees. Elective deferrals are not considered employer contributions for the purpose of tax deductions.	No
Catch-Up Contributions**—Participants who are 50 and older by the end of the plan year may contribute an additional $1,000 per year to their 401(k) plan, up to an additional $5,000 in 2006, when increases in the catch-up limit will be indexed in $500 increments. Catch-up contributions will not be subject to any otherwise applicable limitation on contributions. Matching contributions to catch-up contributions are subject to the nondiscrimination rules and other limits that normally apply to matching contributions.	Yes
Top Heavy Minimum Contribution—Prior to 2002, matching contributions could not count toward the minimum top heavy contribution if they were used to pass the ACP test. Effective in 2002, matching contributions may be counted toward the minimum top heavy contribution, *even if used in an ACP test.*	Yes

Plan Provisions—Vesting, Retirement Planning, Rollovers and Loans Note: Except where indicated, provision is required (** optional provision)	Amendment Required?
Vesting for Employer's Matching Contributions—6-year graded vesting schedule (to permit 20% vesting beginning in a participant's second year of service) or 3-year cliff vesting. Matching contributions in all 401(k) plans, top heavy or otherwise, are subject to the same vesting rules.	Yes
Employer-Provided Retirement Planning—Prior to 2002 there was no specific tax exclusion for the value of employer-provided retirement planning. In 2002, "qualified retirement planning services" are a tax-free fringe benefit for employees and their spouses.	No
Rollover Availability**—Rollovers of post-tax contributions will be allowed as long as the plans accepting post-tax rollovers segregate the amounts from other rollovers.	Yes
Rollover Acceptance**—401(a) qualified plans, 403(b) plans, 457 plans and IRAs may make and accept rollovers to/from such plans. 401(k) and 403(b) plans may combine in one record-keeping source rollovers from 401(a), 403(b), 457, and traditional and conduit IRAs. 457 plans will be required to keep separate recordkeeping accounts for 401(a) and 403(b) rollovers.	Yes
Rollover of Hardship Withdrawals—No portion of a hardship withdrawal, including taxable hardship withdrawals from sources other than salary deferrals, can be rolled over.	Yes
Hardship Withdrawal Suspensions—Participants are required to suspend their elective deferral contributions for a *minimum* of 6 months when a 401(k) hardship payment amount is determined using the "safe harbor" method under the law.	Yes
Spousal Rollovers—Beginning in 2002, a spouse can roll a death benefit to an IRA, another 401(a) qualified plan, a 403(b) plan, or a governmental 457 plan.	Yes
Plan Loans for Owner-Employees**—Prohibited transaction rules are amended to allow plan loans to be made to Owner-Employees without requiring prohibited transaction exemptions.	Yes

Plan Provisions—Distributions and Testing Note: Except where indicated, provision is required (** optional provision)	Amendment Required?
Involuntary Cash-Out Provision**—The amount may be increased to $5,000.	Yes
Applicable Involuntary Cash-Out Balance**—A plan may disregard rollover contributions and related earnings when determining whether an employee's account balance may be involuntarily cashed-out instead of using the total vested amount to determining whether an automatic cash out can be made.	Yes
Anti-Cutback Relief**—Defined contribution plans may eliminate forms of payment available to accrued account balances, as long as certain conditions are met. In addition, a defined contribution plan may accept a transfer from another defined contribution plan even though it does not provide all the forms of distribution previously available under the sending plan, as long as specified conditions are met.	Yes
Section 401(a)(9) Required Distribution**—Companies will have the option to either provide that, for non-5%-owners, the "required beginning date" for required distributions is defined as April 1 of the calendar year following the calendar year in which the participant attains age 70½ (the current provision); or to provide that non-5%-owners may select the "required beginning date" as April 1 of the calendar year following *the later of* (1) the calendar year following the calendar year in which the participant attains age 70½; or (2) the calendar year in which the participant retires.	Yes

Plan Provisions—Distributions and Testing (Cont'd) Note: Except where indicated, provision is required (** optional provision)	Amendment Required?
Elimination of the Same Desk Rule—Distributions of elective contributions made after 12/31/01 will be permitted under certain circumstances, including "severance of employment." A severance of employment occurs when a participant ceases to be employed by the employer that maintains the plan. Effective in 2002, 401(k) distributions are available if the employee continues at the same job when there is a change in the employer (technically a "severance from employment").	No
Top Heavy and Key Employee Determination—For Top Heavy Determination, effective in 2002, although the 5-year look-back period applies to in-service distributions (including hardship withdrawals), event distributions for only the previous year will have to be included. For Key Employee Determination, effective in 2002 there will be a 1-year look-back period.	Yes
Safe Harbor Exemption**—Most plans that use ADP/ACP testing safe harbor provisions will be exempt from top heavy testing.	Yes

Please Note: The information provided is intended as general information and should not be construed as legal advice or a legal opinion on any specific facts or circumstances. Although it includes plan changes considered important in 2002, it is not all-encompassing. The information is not intended to be a substitute for obtaining advice from your own accountant, tax professional or legal counsel. In addition, this table is not intended for duplication or distribution without prior permission.

Prepared by: Linda M. Shashinka, Employee Benefits Attorney

KEY INDUSTRY DATA SOURCES

WEBSITES:

Internal Revenue Service: Employee Retirement Plan Information	*www.irs.gov/ep*
Department of Labor: Retirement Plans, Benefits & Savings	*www.dol.gov/dol/topic/retirement/index.htm*
Profit Sharing/401(k) Council of America	*www.psca.org*
ERISA Industry Committee	*www.eric.org*
Employee Benefits Research Institute	*www.ebri.org*
International Foundation of Employee Benefit Plans	*www.ifebp.org*
American Benefits Council	*www.americanbenefitscouncil.org*
401(k) HelpCenter	*www.401khelpcenter.com*
401k/403b Advocate	*www.timyounkin.com*
403bwise	*www.403bwise.com*
MPower Cafe	*www.mpowercafe.com*
SPARK	www.sparkusa.org
BenefitsLink	*www.benefitslink.com*

World at Work	*www.worldatwork.org*
The Center For Due Diligence	*www.cfdd@401kduediligence.com*
The 401(k) Wire (requires a paid subscription)	*www.401(k)wire.com*
Investment Company Institute	*www.ici.org*
Institute of Management and Administration	*www.ioma.com*
Morningstar	*www.morningstar.com*
Plan Sponsor Magazine	*www.plansponsor.com*
CFO Magazine	*www.cfo.com*
Pension & Investments	*www.pionline.com*
DC News	*www.dcnews.com*

SAMPLE INVESTMENT POLICY
STATEMENT SOURCE

◆

Chicago (August 24, 2001)—The Profit Sharing/401(k) Council of America (PSCA) is pleased to offer another solution to defined contribution plan sponsors by providing a best practices illustration of an investment policy statement for plan sponsors wishing to develop a written investment policy statement for their plan. PSCA has also developed a white paper describing the role of a written investment policy statement in the defined contribution investment process and discussing the advantages and concerns with adopting a written investment policy statement. The model and the white paper are available at:

http://www.psca.org/ips.html.

SPARK RFP

✦

The RFP Guide was developed by SPARK to assist plan sponsors in evaluating and/or selecting service providers for their defined contribution plan, especially their 401(k) plan. Since its inception in 1997, the RFP Guide has gained widespread acceptance within the industry and has been widely acclaimed as the industry standard for RFP requests. The Society is promoting widespread use of this tool to enable service providers to prepare consistent responses to the requests of plan sponsors, resulting in reduced response time and more accurate evaluations.

The 2nd Edition of the RFP Guide can be obtained by completing the following request form. It is available to all SPARK members at no cost as a membership benefit. Other service providers and plan sponsors may obtain a copy of the Guide for a fee of $100.

www.rgwuelfing.com/guide or *www.sparkusa.org*

PSCA Plan Cost Disclosure Worksheet

Service Provider Name: _____ Plan Assets: _____ Prepared On (Date): _____

Number of Plan Participants: _____   Number of Eligible Employees: _____

EXPENSE TYPE	TYPICAL METHOD OF FEE CALCULATION	TOTAL PLAN COST	TOTAL COMPANY COST	TOTAL COST
ONE-TIME FEES				
Startup Education Program	Person-based			
Startup Enrollment Expense	Person-based			
Conversion Fee	Flat fee			
Installation Fee	Flat fee and/or person-based			
One-Time Fund Fee	Flat fee per fund			
Plan Document/IRS Filing Fee	Flat fee			
Consultant	Hourly			
ERISA Attorney	Hourly			
Total One-Time Fees				

ONGOING FEES		TOTAL PLAN COST	TOTAL COMPANY COST	TOTAL YEARLY COST
Fund-Related Investment Expenses	Asset-based (See chart, page 209)			
Annuity Fee	Asset-based			
Comission	Asset-based per transaction			
Front-End Load	Asset-based per transaction			
Management Fee	Asset-based			
Trustee Fee	Asset-based			
Wrap Expense	Asset-based			
Administration/Recordkeeping Fee	Person-based or asset-based			
Ongoing Education Program	Person-based			
Ongoing Enrollment Expense	Person-based			
Balance Inquiry Expense	Transaction-based			
Distribution Expense	Transaction-based			
Investment Transfer Expense	Transaction-based			
Loan Origination Fee	Transaction-based			
Annual Audit Fee	Flat fee			
Annual Loan Maintenance Fee	Flat fee per loan			
Discrimination Testing Expense	Flat fee and/or person-based			
Fidelity Bond Premium	Flat fee			
Fiduciary Insurance Premium	Flat Fee			
Fund Fee	Flat fee			
Signature Ready Form 5500 Fee	Flat fee			
Consultant	Hourly			
ERISA Attorney	Hourly			
Out of Pocket Expenses	Reimbursement for actual costs			
QDRO Charge	Varied methods of calculation			
Total Ongoing Fees				

ONGOING FUND-RELATED INVESTMENT EXPENSES

	Expense Ratio	12(b)1 Fees %	Sub-account Transfer Credits	Assets in Fund	Total Plan Cost	Total Company Cost	Total Yearly Cost
Fund 1	(+	+	)x				
Fund 2	(+	+	)x				
Fund 3	(+	+	)x				
Fund 4	(+	+	)x				
Fund 5	(+	+	)x				
Fund 6	(+	+	)x				
Fund 7	(+	+	)x				

Enter costs in Fund-Related Investment Expenses on page 208. Include addition pages for additional funds, if necessary.

EXPENSE TYPE	TYPICAL METHOD OF FEE CALCULATION	

TERMINATION FEES AND SURRENDER CHARGES (Note: It is important to know these fees and their methods of calculation when evaluating a plan service provider. However, it is difficult to calculate the actual cost of such fees in advance. Use this protion of the worksheet to identify the specific asset-based percentages, person-based fees and flat fees that are used in termination and surrender charge cost calculations.)

Annuity or Stabel Value/GIC Contract Termination Surrender Charges	Asset-based	
Annuity or Stable Value/GIC Participant Transfer or Termination Surrender Charges	Asset-based	
Back-End Load	Asset-based per transaction	
Individual Fund Termination Fee	Asset-based	
Full Plan Termination Charge	Asset-based and/or person-based	
One-Time Plan Termination Fee	Flat fee	

There may be expenses not included on this worksheet. Be sure to ask potential plan providers to list any additional expenses. In addition, not all of the services listed on this worksheet can be delivered by one provider. For example, the fidelity bond will not be provided by the company that invests your plan assets.

Prepared by the Profit Sharing/401(k) Council of America (PSCA)
10 South Riverside Plaze, Suite 1610, Chicago, IL 60606.   312.441.8550.   312.441.8559(FAX)
www.psca.org   pasc@psca.org.

Morningstar Mutual Fund
Data Expense

MORNINGSTAR CATEGORY	EXPENSE RATIO (%)	NUMBER OF FUNDS
GROWTH		
Large Cap	1.45	1,083
Mid Cap	1.55	702
Small Cap	1.64	560
BLEND		
Large Blend	1.22	1,372
Large Blend (Index)*	.68	194
Large Blend (Enhanced Index Fund)*	1.14	62
Mid Cap Blend	1.36	265
Mid Cap Blend (Index)*	.64	29
Mid Cap Blend (Enhanced Index)*	1.19	5
Small Cap Blend	1.41	272
Small Cap Blend (Index)*	.79	30
Small Cap Blend (Enhanced Index)*	1.10	6
FIXED INCOME:		
Government Bond		
Long Government	1.12	64
International Government	1.16	303
Short Government	1.01	135
General Bond		
Long Term Bond	1.05	116
International Term Bond	.99	670
Short Term Bond	.89	252
Ultrashort Bond	.93	94
Specialty Bond		
Emerging Markets Bond	1.62	45
High Yield Bond	1.29	381
Multisector Bond	1.42	180
International Bond	1.35	137
HYBRID		
Domestic Hybrid	1.27	856
International Hybrid	1.55	60

MORNINGSTAR CATEGORY	EXPENSE RATIO (%)	NUMBER OF FUNDS
INTERNATIONAL		
Foreign Stock	1.64	909
World Stock	1.78	320
Europe Stock	1.84	194
Diversified Pacific/Asia Stock Pacific Stock	2.21	63
Pacific/Asia Ex-Japan Stock Pacific Stock	2.14	95
Japan Stock	1.67	59
Diversified Emerging Markets	2.08	190
Latin America Stock	2.07	38
SPECIALTY		
Precious Metals	2.09	39
National Resources	1.69	76
Technology	1.75	397
Utilities	1.44	98
Health	1.74	171
Financial	1.67	118
Real Estate	1.64	155
Communication	1.56	57

*Large Cap Blend, Mid Cap Blend and Small Cap Blend:

Ran a search by:
1. Morningstar Category (Large/Mid/Small Blend) & Special Criteria (Index)
2. Morningstar Category (Large/Mid/Small Blend) & Special Criteria (Enhanced Index)

Index: A fund that tracks a particular index and attempts to match returns. While an index typically has a much larger portfolio than a mutual fund, the fund's management may study the index's movements to develop a representation sampling and match sectors proportionately.

Enhanced Index: Like the index fund, this group includes funds that attempt to match an index's performance. Unlike an index fund, however, enhanced index funds attempt to better the index by either adding value or reducing volatility through selective stock pickings.

Source: Morningstar Principia Pro (through 2/28/02)
For illustrative purposes only

213

LIST OF LEADING SERVICE PROVIDERS

PROVIDER NAME	PHONE	WEB SITE
The 401(k) Company	(800) THE-401K	www.the401k.com
ABN AMRO Asset Management	(800) 224-8719	www.abnamro401k.com
ADP	(800) 432-401K	www.adp401k.com
American Express Asset Management Group	(800) 437-0600	www.americanexpress.com/retirement
American Funds	(800) 421-0180	www.retirement.americanfunds.com
American United Life Insurance (AUL)	(800) 923-2732	www.aul.com/retirement
Charles Schwab Corporate Services	(877) 456-0777	www.charlesschwab.com/retirement
CIGNA Retirement & Investment Services	(800) 574-0615	www.cigna.com/professional/plans/retirement
Delaware Investments	(888) 323-6287	www.delawareinvestments.com/institutional
Diversified Investment Advisors	(800) 770-6797	www.divinvest.com
Equitable Life	(212) 314-5137	www.equitable.com/retirement/employers.html
Fidelity Advisor	(800) 684-5254	http://advisorexpress.fidelity.com/cgi-bin/client
Fidelity Investments	(800) 343-3548	www.300.fidelity.com/employer.shtml
Firstar	See US Bank	http://gettingthere.usbank.com
First Union	(800) 733-8812	www.firstunion.com/retirement
Franklin Templeton	(800) 527-2020	www.franklin-templeton.com
Great-West	(800) 338-4015, ext. 3068	www.gwla.com/benefits
Guardian	(800) 799-4015	www.guardianretirement.com
Hartford Life Insurance	(800) 874-2502	www.thehartford.com/prod_serv/retire_pro/index.html
ING Aetna Financial Services	(888) 238-6243	www.ing-usa.com
Invesco Retirement	(800) 538-6370	www.invescofunds.com/Retirement/RetirementCenter.asp
Invesmart	(877) 934-4015	www.invesmart.com
Lincoln Financial Group	(877) 275-5462	www.lfg.com
Manulife Financial	(877) 346-8378	www.my401ksales.com

PROVIDER NAME	PHONE	WEB SITE
Mass Mutual Retirement	(800) 228-2479	www.massmutual.com/retire
Merrill Lynch	(609) 274-9678	www.businesscenter.ml.com
MetLife	(800) 633-9280	www.metlife.com
Minnesota Life	(651) 665-3500	www.minnesotamutual.com/products/ pension/pension.html
MFS Investment Management	(800) 343-2829	www.mfs.com/retirement/index.jhtml
Mutual of Omaha	(402) 351-7600	www.mutualofomaha.com/retirement/ index.html
Nationwide Financial	(800) 367-5939	www.bestofamerica.com
New York Life Investment Management	(800) 695-8744	www.nylim.com/retirement
Oppenheimer Funds	(212) 323-0200	http://www.oppenheimerfunds.com/ navigation/investors/frame/ frame_retirementPlanning.jhtml
Pan-American Life	(877) 939-4550	www.401k4u.com
Paychex	(800) 322-7292	www.paychex.com
Principal Financial Group	(800) 543-4015	www.principal.com/retirement/biz/ index.htm
Prudential Retirement Services	(800) 353-2847	www.prudential.com/retirement
Putnam Investments	(800) 225-2465	www.putnaminv.com
Scudder Retirement Services	(800) 541-7701	www.scudder.com
Strong	(800) 368-2882	www.estrong.com
Suntrust Bank	(800) 432-4760, ext. 5734	www.suntrust.com/retirement
T. Rowe Price	(800) 638-7890	rps.troweprice.com/gliIndex/0,,,00.html
Transamerica Retirement	(888) 401-5826	www.ta-retirement.com
US Bank	(612) 681-5052	http://gettingthere.usbank.com
Vanguard Group	(800) 523-1036, ext. 14024	http://institutional.vanguard.com
Wells Fargo	(888) 666-5995	www.wellsfargo.com/retirement_center

ADDITIONAL SOURCES

LIST OF E-401(K) PROVIDERS

www.goldk.com

www.401keasy.com

www.emplanet.com

www.e401k.com

www.ez401k.com

www.impact401k.com

www.fidelitye401k.com

LIST OF WEB-BASED SHOPPING SITES

www.401kexchange.com

www.Search401k.com

www.401konnect.com

GLOSSARY

401(k) Plan: 401(k) is a special kind of profit-sharing plan and the only non-IRA qualified plan that allows employees to defer a portion of their own money (up to 100 percent of earned income or an annual dollar limit of $11,000, whichever is less) on a pre-tax basis. Although most companies make some kind of matching contribution, it is also the only corporate retirement plan that does not require an employer contribution, thus making the sponsor's cost potentially zero.

403(b) Plan: 403(b) plans are only available to non-profit organizations. Employees can contribute up to $11,000 per year on a tax-deferred basis. Just like with a 401(k), an employer can match a portion of participants' contributions to a 403(b) plan. Due to legislative tinkering, 401(k) and 403(b) plans are converging with respect to plan design. One major difference remains,403(b) plans do not have to conduct annual discrimination testing of the kind required by 401(k) plans.

DOL 404(c): In 1992, the Department of Labor issued final regulations designed to provide limited fiduciary relief to plan sponsors in participant investment-directed plans. Specifically in a 404(c) compliant plan, the sponsor is not liable for investment losses resulting from the participant's control. In order to satisfy 404(c) requirements, the regulations state that the plan must meet certain conditions.

457(b) Plan: Section 457 of the IRS Code allows certain governmental organizations to sponsor a plan whereby employees can defer up to $11,000 on a pre-tax basis for retirement. The types of organizations include state, city, state agency or political subdivision such as a school district, and any organization exempt from federal income tax (including non-profits) except for a church or synagogue.

12b-1 Fee: A fee (named for a Securities and Exchange Commission rule) charged by mutual fund which is used to pay for fund marketing costs, such as advertising, sales material and commissions.

ADP/ACP: Two 401(k) non-discrimination tests—average deferral percentage test (ADP) and average contribution percentage test (ACP)—which are used to ensure that no plan discriminates in favor of highly-compensated employees in the areas of contributions and benefits.

adoption agreement: The adoption agreement controls the main plan design elements, and the employer can customize the plan by selecting among a well-defined set of options.

alliance: The investment alliance concept allows sponsors and participants to select investments from a cross-section of mutual fund families through a single record-keeping platform.

annuity contracts: Many insurance companies use brand-name mutual funds as investment options within their 401(k) products. The underlying fund is wrapped in an insurance company's group variable annuity shell for legal and marketing purposes. These funds are not required to be registered with the SEC.

annualized return: A mathematical means of expressing a rate of return for a period greater or less than one year in terms of twelve months.

automatic or "negative" enrollment: Also referred to as "negative enrollment", allows an employer to automatically enroll all eligible employees without first requiring them to fill out a salary reduction form.

basis point: A fraction of a percent (e.g. 100 basis points is the same as 1%; 100 basis point are equal to 1%).

beta: A mathematical means of measuring a stock's relative volatility in relationship to the rest of the stock market.

black-out: A period of time during the conversion period where certain plan actions are not permitted to occur because insufficient information is available to process the requested action. Normally, a black-out period is imposed at the beginning of a plan conversion and lasts until individual participant account records and assets have been reconciled by the new recordkeeper.

bundled: A streamlined service delivery model in which all core services are delivered by a single provider. "Bundled" is a less than precise term. Generally, if a participant only "sees" one service provider, then the product is bundled.

collective trust: A collective trust is an investment vehicle created by pooling assets of unrelated retirement plans. They are most often managed by the trust departments of banks. Unlike mutual funds, they are not registered with the SEC. Sometimes referred to as a "commingled pool."

compliance: A plan is in compliance when it is administered exactly as the plan document is written, it completes all necessary testing and government filings and distributes all legally required information to participants.

daily valuation: Participants' accounts are updated based on the day's closing market prices.

defined benefit (DB): Defined benefit plans represent a company's "promise to pay" a retirement benefit based on variables such as average income, years of service, and retirement age. In these highly regulated plans, company contributions are actuarially determined each year on the basis of the benefit formula. With a DB plan, you can calculate today exactly what your benefit will be at the time of your retirement.

defined contribution (DC): Unlike with a Defined Benefit plan, the amount available from a Defined Contribution plan is not known until retirement. In a DC plan, a participant's account balance is determined by the level of employer and employee contributions and the investment return over time. The participant bears all the investment risk in a DC plan.

discrimination testing (ADP/ACP): See ADP/ACP above.

diversified: According to the Sec, a mutual fund cannot advertise itself as "diversified" unless it is able to meet its "75-5-10" rule. Seventy-five percent of total assets must be invested in securities issued by companies other than the investment company itself. No more than 5% of total assets can be invested in any one corporation's securities. No more than 10% of an outside corporation's common stock can be owned by the investment company.

economic growth and tax relief reconciliation act (EGTRRA): The Economic Growth and Tax Relief Reconciliation Act of 2001, enacted June 7, 2001, includes numerous changes to rules for pensions and benefits. (See Appendix for summary of the EGTRRA's main provisions.)

ERISA: Passed in 1974, and enforced by the Department of Labor, ERISA was designed to protect the interests of retirement plan participants. ERISA establishes employee eligibility, vesting, minimum funding requirements, administration of plans and plan assets, and disclosure and reporting of plan information to participants and beneficiaries.

expense ratio: The expense ratio is the percentage of plan assets paid for fund operation, distribution, and management fees.

explicit fees: Explicit fees are charges that are billed directly either to the plan sponsor or to plan participants.

fiduciary: Any person who has discretion or control over a plan's assets or who has discretionary authority for managing the plan.

forfeitures: Forfeitures refer to the unvested employer contributions "forfeited" back to the plan after a participant leaves.

hardship withdrawal: 401(k) plans allow for the early distribution of retirement money due to extreme financial hardship. Hardship withdrawals are granted if the participant meets certain criteria.

implicit fees: Implicit or asset-based fees are derived as a function of the plan assets.

individually designed plan: A plan tailored specifically to meet the needs of the plan sponsor. No pre-approval by the IRS exists. For approval, the document must be submitted by the plan sponsor's legal representative.

institutional: Refers to buyers such as retirement plans, endowments, corporations, foundations, etc.

Investment policy statement (IPS): A formal investment criteria used to guide fiduciaries in the evaluation, selection, and monitoring of investments. An IPS is a blueprint or map, created by the plan sponsor to determine which investments are appropriate for the plan. A thorough IPS specifies the investment objectives of the plan and the way investments are selected and monitored.

load funds: Front- or back-end loads, transaction costs charged when a participant buys shares of a fund either going into the plan (front-end) or exiting a fund (back-end).

money purchase plan: A Money Purchase Plan allows a company to deduct up to 25 percent of aggregate employee compensation subject to annual limit of $40,000. Unlike a profit-sharing contribution that can fluctuate from year to year, a money purchase contribution percentage is mandatory and can only be changed by formally amending the plan.

mutual fund: A mutual fund pools money from many investors and invests it on the basis of a clearly stated objective. Some invest primarily in stocks, some in bonds, and some in combination.

net asset value: Also known as "price per share"; the value of a fund's assets divided by the number of outstanding shares.

nonqualified Plan: Nonqualified plans fall outside the scope of government regulations and, by definition, do not have to follow the complex and sometimes cumbersome rules of qualified plans. These plans are usually established for top executives as supplemental retirement plans over and above the qualified plans.

plan administration: This refers to the nuts-and-bolts operation of a plan, including payroll, tax compliance, implementation of participant-directed activity and distribution processing.

plan document: The plan document describes the design features and the operations of the plan.

plan sponsor: The company sponsoring the retirement plan is known as the "plan sponsor."

profit sharing plan: The key feature of profit-sharing plans is flexibility. Each year a company decides how much to contribute from 0 to 25 percent of each eligible employee's compensation subject to an annual dollar limit of $40,000. The sponsor can link the contribution to some measure of company performance, such as "profit," but it is not required to. It could even forgo making an annual contribution if sufficient funds weren't available.

prototype plan document: An Internal Revenue Service-approved plan sponsored by a bank, insurance company, mutual fund or other organization approved by the IRS that is made available for adoption by a client of the sponsoring organization.

qualified domestic relations order (QDRO): A judgment, decree or other order made pursuant to a state domestic relations law that creates a right for an alternate payee to receive some or all of a participant's benefit in a qualified plan.

qualified plan: Qualifed plans receive preferential tax treatment under the tax code. Money in a qualified plan grows tax-deferred until withdrawal. Employees receive an immediate tax deduction for their contributions to these plans and employers receive a deduction for the administrative costs of maintaining them. In exchange for this privileged tax treatment, qualified plans have to abide by ERISA.

recordkeeping: Recordkeeping refers to the tracking of employer and employee contributions and the calculation of investment gains and losses and dividend distributions. In addition, recordkeeping includes the complementary technology systems supporting the delivery of plan information to both plan participants and sponsors.

registered investment product: Investments such as mutual funds that are required to be registered with the SEC.

required minimum distributions: Provisions requiring the distribution of at least a minimal amount of retirement benefit based on the age and life expectancy of the employee and his/her beneficiary.

retail: Refers to individual, as opposed to institutional, investors.

safe harbor 401(k): Any size company may consider this option. There are two contribution alternatives a company can consider for Safe Harbor 401(k). The plan can make an immediately vested 3 percent contribution to all NHCEs who are eligible to participate in the 401(k) plan. Alternatively, the employer may elect to make immediately vested matching contributions to NHCEs equal to 100 percent of the first 3 percent of employee contributions, plus 50 percent of the next 2 percent of employee contributions.

Security Exchange Commission (SEC): Commission created by Congress to regulate the securities markets and protect investors. It is composed of five commissioners appointed by the President of the United States and approved by the Senate.

separate account: A separate account is a customized portfolio in which the assets are held by an independent trustee or custodian and are designed to meet the needs of a particular investor or group of investors. For example, an insurance company may create a separate account (as opposed to the general account) and use the assets to buy shares of a retail mutual fund.

SIMPLE IRA Plan: The SIMPLE IRA is designed to offer greater income deferral opportunities than individual retirement accounts (IRA), with fewer restrictions and administrative requirements than traditional pension or profit-sharing plans. With this type of plan, an employee can elect to have a percentage of his compensation up to $7,000 set aside in an IRA on a pre-tax basis. Unlike a qualified salary-reduction arrangement, the employer must make "matching" contributions. That is, the employer must make contributions to an employee's SIMPLE account up to 3 percent of the employee's compensation. Alternatively, instead of making "matching" employee contributions, the employer can simply contribute a flat 2 percent of "compensation" for every eligible employee whether the employee elects to contribute or not.

Simplified Employer Pension (SEP): In a SEP-IRA, the employer contributes the same percentage to each participant's IRA. This plan is designed for sole proprietors and small businesses, where the employer decides annually what percentage of salary will be contributed, from 0 to 15% up to a dollar maximum of $30,000. A SEP can exclude from eligibility people with less than three years of employment. Loans are not permitted, and employees are vested immediately upon joining the plan. Part-time employees are eligible for the plan once they meet the three-year eligibility period.

Summary Plan Description (SPD): The Summary Plan Description (SPD) describes in simple language the main provisions of the plan and must be distributed to plan participants.

stable value: Stable value accounts are like a CD paying a guaranteed rate of interest.

standard deviation: Indicates the volatility of a fund's total returns. Unlike alpha, beta and R-squared (R2) which rely on a fund's relationship to the market, the standard deviation is fund specific.

target-benefit: A target-benefit plan combines many features of a defined benefit plan, yet at its core it remains a defined contribution plan. As in a defined benefit plan, the employer's contributions are calculated yearly on the basis of a participant's salary, years of service, and other actuarial assumptions. Unlike a defined benefit, however, the participant assumes 100 percent of the investment risk, and the retirement balance is not known in advance but is determined by the participant's investment selections and their performance. The maximum contribution limitation is 25 percent. Because they use a funding formula, which weights salary and years of service, target-benefit plans favors older, more highly paid employees.

trustee: A trustee receives, holds, and distributes plan assets according to the plan provisions, and ensures the accurate transmission and allocation of investment contributions.

unbundled: The plan sponsor selects a separate organization to perform each critical task.

vesting: Employer contributions may be subject to a "vesting" schedule, which refers to the "ownership" of employer contributions.

wrap fee: "Wrap" fees are common expense-recovery mechanisms in the start-up and small-plan marketplace (under $10 million of total assets) an are usually associated with insurance companies. With this type of fee, the insurance company establishes separate investment accounts using retail mutual funds as the underlying investment vehicle. The separate account then "wraps" an additional fee over and above the cost of the underlying investment.

INDEX